I Know How to Live,
I Know How to Die

I Know How to Live, I Know How to Die

The Teachings of Dadi Janki:
A warm, radical, and life-affirming view
of who we are, where we come from,
and what time is calling us to do

Neville Hodgkinson

MANTRA
BOOKS

Winchester, UK
Washington, USA

First published by Mantra Books, 2015
Mantra Books is an imprint of John Hunt Publishing Ltd., Laurel House, Station Approach,
Alresford, Hants, SO24 9JH, UK
office1@jhpbooks.net
www.johnhuntpublishing.com
www.mantra-books.net

For distributor details and how to order please visit the 'Ordering' section on our website.

Text copyright: Neville Hodgkinson 2014

ISBN: 978 1 78535 013 9
Library of Congress Control Number: 2014959598

A CIP catalogue record for this book is available from the British Library.

Design: Lee Nash

Printed in the USA by Edwards Brothers Malloy

We operate a distinctive and ethical publishing philosophy in all
areas of our business, from our global network of authors to
production and worldwide distribution.

CONTENTS

Author's Note

This book is based on the teachings of the Brahma Kumaris (BK), a woman-led spiritual training organisation founded in India in the mid-1930s. It especially features aspects of the life and thought of Dadi (elder sister) Janki, a founding member who now leads the organisation globally. Dadi was resident for many years in the UK, where I first met her in 1981. A highly accomplished "yogi", Dadi has inspired many to take up a life conducive to spiritual growth and awareness.

The book offers understandings that support as well as challenge some aspects of traditional wisdom concerning the soul and God. It explores territory well beyond the boundaries imposed by scientific materialism, which shapes so much of modern-day culture. It does so, however, in a way that attempts to draw on findings at the frontiers of science, addressing the intellectual implications as well as subjective, devotional meaning for our lives.

Special thanks to Sister Jayanti, BK European Director, for her patient support and guidance; to Judy Rodgers, for proposing the "living and dying" theme, and for her unwavering encouragement; to Andrew Powell and Liz Hodgkinson, for their valuable suggestions as to content and style; to Marcus and Mary Braybrooke, for helping to keep me grounded during tough times, and to Marcus for writing the preface; to Jon Russell, for permission to use extracts from the *Door Ke Musafir* songs; and to all at the Global Retreat Centre, Oxford, for their love and friendship.

Neville Hodgkinson worked for many years as full-time medical and science correspondent of a number of newspapers in the UK, including The Sunday Times *and* Daily Mail. *He is the author of* Will to be Well – the Real Alternative Medicine *(Hutchinson,1984) and* AIDS:

vii

The Failure of Contemporary Science *(Fourth Estate, 1996). He begun practising Raja Yoga in 1981 and 20 years ago decided to dedicate his life to the BK movement. He lives at a retreat centre near Oxford.*

Preface

This is a beautiful book about a beautiful soul. It tells the story of Dadi Janki, who is Head of the Brahma Kumaris World Spiritual University, and outlines her teaching, which has inspired people in every continent.

From an early age, Dadi Janki was searching for God. At the age of 19 she met Dada Lekhraj (later known as Brahma Baba) and as their eyes met, she had a sense of light and love. She joined Brahma Baba's small group of followers, who in 1950 settled at Mount Abu in Northern India. In the early 1970s she was asked to go to Europe to share the message there, but Europe was too small for her and over the years she has travelled constantly across the world.

Yet although so often on the move, she has an inner stillness. It is the fruit of spending long hours in the presence of the Supreme Soul, who "comes as a Mother and a Father to find His children and take them into His arms to refresh and renew them". In deep meditation, she says, one recovers an awareness of the soul's original purity. This reminds me of St Paul's words that as the veil of ignorance is removed, and we behold the glory of God, we are changed into the same image – from glory to glory. (2 Corinthians 3, 18)

Dadi recognises that the happiness which comes from sharing with the Supreme is not "just for us, but for the whole of humanity, and preparing us for lives of service".

The happiness that radiates from a life of surrender to God and of service to others means, Dadi says, that "we will die in happiness. If our hands are always giving, always bestowing, joy will be ours in death as well as life".

Just as Dadi Janki has been deeply influenced by Brahma Baba, so Neville Hodgkinson, the author of this inspiring book, has been influenced by Dadi Janki. In sharing Dadi's teaching, he is also sharing his own growing realisation of the love of the Supreme Soul. The book, therefore, in the end, is not so much about Dadi , as about ourselves and "God's longing for us to rediscover our original nature as God's much loved children".

It is a message that resonates with me as a Christian – even if I do not share all the philosophical framework. Rumi said that "the religion of love is the message of all religions". I pray that this book will help many people rediscover for themselves their divine beauty and by sharing this bring light to a dark world.

Marcus Braybrooke
Rev Dr Marcus Braybrooke, President of the World Congress of Faiths

Introduction

During the post-world-war period in which I grew up, science seemed as important to maintaining peace as to improving our mastery of the physical world. My generation was very aware of how religious and quasi-religious dogma and superstition were capable of distorting human minds, to the point of giving rise to unimaginable cruelties. The materialistic scientific paradigm, with its focus on objectivity, measurement, and repeatability, appeared to offer protection against such tragedies.

As a newspaper reporter, I specialised in writing about science and medicine partly because of my own appreciation for the scientific method and distaste for religious fanaticism and dogma.

About half way through my career, however, I underwent a visionary experience that marked the beginning of a new phase in my life and thought. I embraced an ascetic path, known as Raja Yoga, whose central thrust is to quieten "noise" from mental conditioning and the senses, in order to foster the experience of love and wisdom from a realm of awareness that lies beyond the brain.

Dadi Janki, the essence of whose life and thought this book presents, has now been my guide on this path for more than 30 years, along with other teachers of the Brahma Kumaris World Spiritual University.

The practice immediately gave me much joy, improving my ability to negotiate the daily vicissitudes of newspaper work with equanimity and strength.

However, it also created internal conflict. It involved working with a spiritual paradigm that did not fit the materialistic worldview with which I had lived previously.

Today, I consider it my good fortune to have been able to absorb a different story of reality – one that has not only enabled me to access a happiness that previously eluded me, but which may also help science put together a more complete picture of how the world works.

Limitations of scientific materialism

Paradigms are important. The word comes from ancient Greek, meaning "shown beside". A paradigm is a mental map or framework that helps us interpret what is going on, whether in the laboratory or in life, and consequently guides our actions.

The achievements of scientific materialism as a mental map are all around us, in terms of detailed understanding of material processes, and technological advances often harnessing great physical power.

The limitations of the paradigm have become increasingly apparent, however. Current scientific theories and methods have been unable to account for the emergence of either life, or consciousness. Nor do they acknowledge the intertwined nature of matter and mind, indicated by the branch of physics known as quantum mechanics, as well as by everyday experience in which our thoughts can have an immediate and far-reaching impact on our physical functioning.

Paradoxically, scientific materialism's focus on external realities can also weaken the objectivity that it prizes so highly. Researchers who neglect their inner world become unaware of how much their mental and emotional needs are influencing their observations.

Perhaps most damagingly, when our mental map tells us we are isolated lumps of matter fighting for survival in a material world, it tends to make us forgetful of the consequences of our actions on the planet, its elements, and our own bodies, as well as on each other.

A fresh story of reality

The different understanding I have taken on board is that the roots of our being lie within a non-material realm outside space and time. Each one of us is an eternal soul, and each soul has the deepest imaginable, indescribably beautiful peace as our original nature.

Furthermore, this peace is always available, providing we keep open the doors of perception that allow us to experience it. The pull of the body, and habitual thought-patterns related to the body, cause us to forget it.

Along with peace, there is love, and bliss. These qualities and experiences are intrinsic to human souls. We become restless and unhappy, and feel unfulfilled, when life and its complications block the experience, and the expression, of the beauty of our transcendent being.

This beauty is our primary reality. As souls, or individuated units of consciousness, we are distinct from the body, although we negotiate the world of time and space through the brain and senses.

The body is not the essence of who we are. The intricacies of our relationship with it have caused us to identify with it, but this is a mistake. The metaphor of a car, and its driver, gives a more accurate picture. No matter how intelligent modern cars are becoming, with their computer-controlled sensors, navigation aids, and so on, they are still not us. It is the same with our bodies. When the soul leaves, the body quickly dissolves into its constituent chemicals.

Non-dualistic view

Scientists and philosophers alike usually dismiss the "dualistic" idea of soul and body – of a "ghost in the machine". They have long argued that however unacceptable it might feel, our world and its inhabitants are all ultimately machine-like.

Now, however, some of the best minds at the frontiers of physics and biology are developing a map of the way things are that avoids philosophical dualism, whilst helping us to understand how the living energy of "soul" may be central to reality.

This view holds that in nature, what we call matter is a projection of what lies within soul. Every material thing, from a particle, to a flower, to a human body, or to the cosmos, takes its form through continuous interaction with a subtle level of reality. It is as though there are hidden, informational blueprints operating the various aspects of the theatre of life. Taken together, these make up the overall drama of existence.

The blueprints are thought to be reflected within immensely refined wave forms that are present in constantly evolving fields. These fields carry the information – "in-formation" – that determines what happens at the material level. They constitute a more basic reality than the relatively simple action-and-reaction descriptions of traditional, so-called classical physics.

The concept of information lies at the heart of this new paradigm, but to be meaningful, information needs both a source, and something to be informed. We can see these subtle, informational fields as a bridge between soul, or spirit, and the material world, to which the information gives form.

Everything is interconnected

This new thinking, sometimes referred to as the consciousness-based paradigm or post-materialist science, looks set to bring some aspects of religious understanding right back into the realm of science. In several disciplines, including biology and neuroscience as well as physics, studies of the interaction of consciousness and matter are moving to centre stage.

In the new paradigm, everything is interconnected. We share a common understanding or "feeling" about the quality of different colours, for example, because of a deep connection between the different wavelength characteristics of the colours, the sensory equipment that enables us to distinguish them, and the consciousness – the "I" – that sees.

As indicated, some physicists have argued that even the elements are at some level mind-like, in the sense that they are capable of both holding and responding to subtle information. The late David Bohm, formerly Professor of Theoretical Physics at Birkbeck College, University of London, was a pioneer of this way of thinking.

Returning to the metaphor of the car and its driver, it is as though the body, with all its senses, is custom-made for the conscient being, the soul, who is to drive it. Certain features of the body (two arms and two legs, for example) are provided by "the soul of Nature" as standard equipment in humans, but our individual genetic inheritance brings huge variation in the detailed finish. DNA, the molecule from which genes are made, once thought to be "the secret of life", may instead comprise a kind of bar code, allowing our body cells to act, repair and renew in accordance with information from a deeper level.

Moreover, scientists have now demonstrated that the brain as well as the body change constantly according to how we use them. The many shades of physical difference ultimately reflect the uniqueness of each soul, and each soul's role, so it is not surprising that we feel more closely identified with our bodies than we do with the cars we drive.

Love's power

As we learn, even individual brain cells (neurons) change their structure, as well as their connectivity. Thinking, learning and acting bring changes in the activity of genes inside the cells, enabling the brain to adapt at a fundamental level.

This principle operates not only with regard to developing new skills such as learning a language or playing the piano, but also to components of our character such as habitual attitudes. People with a positive approach to life show greater than average activity and connectivity within a specific area of the brain connected with such an attitude. Similarly, those who are habitually demoralised or depressed show greater activity within a parallel brain area. Just a few weeks of contemplative practice can downgrade the activity of the brain cells connected with low morale, and upgrade the "happiness" neurons.

Lasting change requires persistent, close attention. It is promoted both by forces that inhibit or destroy old patterns and connections, and by forces that promote new ones.

Love, it seems, can do both. Scientists tell us that when we fall in love, or become parents, massive brain reorganisation takes place. Millions of old neural networks fall away, as millions of new ones form.

Norman Doidge, a New York psychiatrist whose 2007 book *The Brain that Changes Itself* reviews decades of brain research, explains the pros and cons of this process. It reduces the pain of losing previous attachments. It helps two people to mould to each other and shape each other's intentions and perceptions. It also allows us to change our image of ourselves – "for the better, if we have an adoring partner". He adds however that the heightened neuroplasticity that accompanies falling in love helps account for our added vulnerability at such times.

In the light of the consciousness-based paradigm, we can understand that the brain does not change itself. It changes according to how the soul uses it, or allows it to be used by other people or circumstances.

On the path of transformation to which Dadi Janki has dedicated her life, it is inadvisable to "lose oneself" in another person. Even a loving relationship will lead to frustration and hurt if it involves deep attachment, and in today's world that is difficult to avoid. So many partnerships that seemed to offer happiness end in quarrelling and sorrow. Multiple hurts of this kind contribute to a lack of faith in love.

The life journey that Dadi Janki exemplifies has love for God at its heart. God, for the Raj Yogi, is in a sense more real than the world of "things". He is an eternal Being who resides outside space-time, yet holds within Himself the knowledge of everything that happens within the material world. He is also an

Ocean of Love.

The challenge we face is to allow ourselves to open up to this divine love and wisdom, in order to restore our own loving nature to its full expression.

Subtle interaction

In the past, scientists looked closely into the brain to try to find evidence for the soul. They even weighed people, before and immediately after death, to see if there was any difference. Such efforts were in vain, and eventually the materialistic idea, that the brain is solely responsible for our sense of mind and self, came to predominate. It may be, however, that our instruments have simply not been refined enough, to date, to pick up the subtlety of the interaction between soul and body.

An image that helps us to understand how this interaction may work is that of a supertanker out at sea, sailing along under its own steam, with giant on-board engines generating the massive amounts of energy needed to keep pushing it through the water. Suppose the vessel also has an automatic pilot, linked by radio to a controller on a distant shore. With a simple signal, using an almost imperceptible amount of energy, the controller can change the giant tanker's course.

One current theory holds that highly refined structures within brain cells, known as microtubules, may be doing a similar job, able to catch and respond to subtle signals from a realm that lies beyond the physical, as we know it today. We may be receiving clues about the reality of this realm when we dream, seamlessly flitting from one scene to another, transcending the normal limitations of time and space.

People who have "died" clinically, only to be resuscitated some while later, quite often recall experiences of moving away from the body into a mental realm where they know that they still exist, but are no longer subject to the limitations of the gross physical world. Systematic, scientific study of these near-death experiences (NDEs) has provided further independent support for the consciousness-based paradigm. The Dutch cardiologist Pim van Lommel gives a first-class account of this research, put in the context of the new paradigm, in his book *Consciousness Beyond Life – the Science of the Near-Death Experience* (HarperCollins, 2010).

Life-changing brushes with death

Most people who recall an NDE report a sense of passing through different levels of consciousness as they move further and further from the awareness of the body. To begin with, they may find themselves looking down on the body, and the doctors busying around it, and realise to their surprise that it is their own. Some then experience what has come to be known as a life review, in which they see key scenes from the life just lived, especially ones in which they face up to having caused previously unacknowledged hurts to others.

A sense of moving through a tunnel into a realm of pure mind, or divine light, often follows. Angelic figures, and sometimes long-deceased relatives, provide a welcome. Communication is telepathic rather than through sound. Individuals report that they only have to think of a person, to find themselves connected to them. As well as scenes from the past, there are sometimes glimpses of the future.

Love, peace and joy are everywhere in these higher realms, such that there is often a reluctance to return to the body, usually overcome by a feeling of having unfinished business here in the physical world. The subjects also describe wanting to share the glory they glimpsed, and the certainty that death is not the end.

Studies lasting several years have shown that an NDE often brings profound change in the way the person lives subsequently. They may drop their previous worldly aims and ambitions, and seek instead to live a life more conducive to sharing the love and peace they experienced "beyond".

In accordance with the materialistic paradigm, most doctors

and scientists understand the mind as a product of the complexity of the brain. As a result, they tend to be dismissive of such stories, regarding them as imaginative fictions, perhaps created by the brain to ease the death process.

It would not be surprising to find that the brain is involved in altered states of consciousness surrounding death, and near-death, including feelings of transcending the narrow sense of self to which the brain itself gives rise.

However, a growing body of research into the phenomenon, along with publication by brain scientists and others of NDE-like experiences they have undergone themselves, supports the idea that we are conscious agents who exist independently of the brain and body.

A non-mechanical reality

Several decades ago the English physicist, astronomer and mathematician Sir James Jeans predicted that the stream of knowledge was heading towards a non-mechanical reality. "The Universe begins to look more like a great thought than like a great machine," he wrote. Mind and matter, "if not proved to be of similar nature, are at least found to be ingredients of one single system."

He also anticipated the concept of the individual soul, writing "It may well be ... that each individual consciousness ought to be compared to a brain-cell in a universal mind."

Today, whereas society generally tolerates religion if it confines itself to promoting social cohesion and higher values, many people still pejoratively label as "magical thinking" any ideas or phenomena that challenge materialism. They fear it may herald a dangerous throwback to a primitive past.

Yet according to the late John Wheeler, an American theoretical physicist, "There may be no such thing as the 'glittering central mechanism of the universe' to be seen behind a glass wall at the end of the trail. Not machinery but magic may be the better description of the treasure that is waiting."

Scholars from other disciplines are also challenging some of science's fundamental assumptions. Thomas Nagel, a distinguished philosopher, whilst acknowledging the value of the search for objective understanding, highlighted the need for "a major conceptual revolution" to counter materialist dogma in his 2012 book *Mind and Cosmos: Why the Materialist Neo-Darwinian Conception of Nature Is Almost Certainly False* (Oxford University Press).

Living and dying

Dadi Janki does not engage in either scientific or philosophical discourse. For her, the realities of soul, the loss we suffer through over-identification with matter, and the attainments that come through relationship with a divine Source or Supreme Being, are as clear as night and day.

This book describes how she adopted soul-awareness as the basis of her life, and what she learned (and is still learning, after nearly a century of practice) about maintaining peace, love, wisdom and happiness in action and relationship with others.

With such a life, she says, in which she has used her breath, thoughts, time and energy well, death holds no fears. The soul will carry with it the truth restored in it by the Supreme.

Scientists take great pains to test theories, especially new ones, to try to avoid being fooled into believing something that is not true. However, as a wise philosopher has pointed out, there is a second way of being fooled, which is to refuse to believe what is true.

Most of us, consciously and unconsciously, hold science in high regard because of the way it has helped advance our understanding of the world around us.

Time is now calling us to let go of some of the materialistic beliefs we have held dear, in order to enable us to better understand ourselves.

Part 1: Birth

"The mind is not a vessel to be filled, but a fire to be kindled."

– Plutarch

Chapter 1

Bathed in Light

Who has come, who has come
Who has come to the door of my heart
With the tinkle of ankle bells
Who has come*

From her earliest days, Dadi Janki had the feeling that the secret of life would lie in learning about God. She only underwent three years of formal schooling, and for the rest was a devout student of Hindu scriptures, and the *dharma* of putting religious principles into practice. Her father introduced her to many sages and saints and took her on pilgrimages all over India.

None of this satisfied her. She saw many impressive demonstrations of devotional practice, with all sorts of chants, special physical powers, and amazing skills of oratory. However, it seemed rather self-absorbed; and hard work! Children are perceptive and sometimes she was struck by a contrast between what the teachers and holy men said, and how they behaved in private. She did not find the love that her heart told her was somehow of the essence of God.

Until one day, when she was 19, and out walking with her father in her home town of Hyderabad, Sindh, a province in Northern India that became part of Pakistan after the 1947 partition. They came across Dada Lekhraj, a jeweller of high standing in Sindh. She had known him from early childhood, but now something had changed. As he approached, with his gaze meeting hers, she felt transported to some timeless dimension, beyond this material world. It was as if she no longer existed as a bodily being. There was a sense of filling with light – and pure love. In that instant she felt that she had at last found what she had been looking for over all those years.

Soon afterwards, she learned that this transformation in Dada had come about through some visions he had experienced, and that those insights followed a period in which he had made persistent, conscious efforts to become aware of his own divinity, repeatedly reminding himself that he was a soul, distinct from brain and body. It was as though he had prised open the doors of perception that keep most people's everyday consciousness at the mundane level, and a higher awareness, or divine light, had flooded into him.

Darkness in the world

Those were particularly dark days in the world. It was the mid-1930s, between the two terrible wars that convulsed European and other nations. There was a global recession, and many in India lived in great poverty, though the Sindh business community remained relatively prosperous. Britain's imperial role was in steep decline. Religions, once a source of so much communal as well as personal inspiration, seemed to have deteriorated into self-serving vehicles for the exercise of institutional power and control.

Everyone was suffering, but women, in particular, were often at the mercy of inadequate and insecure men. In India, girls were subject to strong traditions of social and religious as well as parental authority. This meant they often had to marry in accordance with the wishes and needs of others, sometimes barely out of childhood; and once married, their husband was supposed to be their lord and master – their guru. When the system operated in a benevolent way, it had its advantages. Where there was a lack of good authority, it could become a vehicle for systematic abuse, resulting in lives of misery and suppression.

Into this darkness, came a light that was to trigger a global revolution.

Just as the young Janki had been transported by the radiance in Dada Lekhraj, many others were experiencing the same. Gatherings were taking place at his home, which held an enormous attraction. It was like moths circling a flame. The women of the community were particularly drawn, and the men, often away from home on business for long periods, were at first happy for their womenfolk to be receiving good company, and uplifting instruction.

This was no ordinary religious *satsang*, however. In the wake of his visions, which he felt were of divine origin, Dada was teaching a radical understanding. It had become clear to him that we were entering a time of transition, in which our world, now tired and old, would be renewed. This would happen at the level of human consciousness first: only then could heaven on earth, the fabled golden age in which human beings would once again live with universal peace, love and joy, replace the hell which so many were experiencing.

Understandings of this kind, involving a repeating cycle of time, lie at the heart of Indian spirituality. However, whereas tradition considers the existing cycle to have thousands of years yet to run, Dada's insight was that the transition from old to new is imminent. He made those drawn to him feel that time was calling each one to make their own, immediate contribution to the process, by letting go of the influence of the past and immersing themselves in divine truth.

Joy of self-transcendence

This would involve a surrender to the will of God, in which they would become so steeped in the joy of self-transcendence that mundane interests and worldly desires would fall away. They would all – men and women – become brides of God, renouncing all forms of selfishness and violence. That meant removing anger, greed, attachment, and the persistent, underlying demands of the ego linked to bodily awareness. They would become free spirits, angels, able to guide the world through upheavals that lay ahead.

The most dramatic call, which was to become the source of great controversy, was to refrain from sexual relations, even within marriage. Even today, many would consider this an unnatural and undesirable option, although tolerance towards different life choices has increased in most parts of the world. In 1930s India, it caused outrage.

When Janki heard and felt this call, she was newly married (albeit against her will) to a young man she hardly knew. The poor fellow was affronted by her longing to join the gathering, and her rejection of conventional married life. For about 18 months, he made her a virtual prisoner at home. He would fly into a rage if he thought she was so much as remembering Dada Lekhraj and the fledgling spiritual community. On occasions he beat her around the head so fiercely that blood matted her hair.

Eventually her father realised he had made a terrible mistake in marrying her off, and helped her escape to Karachi, where the community had moved in 1939 to try to escape the anger in Hyderabad. In fact, for a while, some elders tried even harder to disband them, but eventually they were allowed to continue their lives in peace.

Birth of Brahma

By this time, Dada had developed such a deep conviction of his personal and pivotal role in the task of global transformation that he took the name Brahma, representative of creation in Indian mythology. His understanding was that through him, God was initiating the renewal of consciousness that would recreate the world.

To the community that had grown around him, what mattered was that they felt bathed in an unending spiritual love that enabled them to allow their weaknesses and insecurities to fall away, and aspire towards developing the strength of character that would fit them for the pure new world to follow.

Around 300 stayed together in Karachi until 1950, when they moved to Mount Abu in Rajasthan, India. At the outset, Dada Lekhraj sold his share in his business, and the funds were such as to enable the entire group to live comfortably, in a world of their own, throughout those years. Even during the upheaval that accompanied the partition of India, when hundreds of thousands died, they remained safe, protected by local well-wishers who had recognised the spiritual power and integrity of the community.

Some whole families joined, also contributing significant resources, but the great majority of the 300 who stayed throughout those years were women. Nine of these, all young kumaris (unmarried girls), were appointed trustees and given administrative responsibility. This was later to give rise to the name "Brahma Kumaris" (BKs) by which the movement came to be known, and to this day, women hold the foremost roles, although most BKs now live in their homes with their families. The aim behind this principle was and is to help the mothers and kumaris to develop self-respect. In those days, people in India generally had little regard for women, in comparison to men; they thought women were only useful for looking after the home and children.

Hearts and minds with One

Brahma Baba had been such an inspiration that when he passed on in 1969, many thought that would be the end of the BKs. Instead, the spiritual university has flourished and now has thousands of teachers spread across India and the world, benefiting millions.

The reason for this success, Dadi Janki says, is that the founding community learned in those intense early years how to connect their hearts and minds to God. Not to a human being, but to the "One above" – the One who, unlike the human family, never loses His way. The One who remains an Ocean of Love and Truth. The One who restores love and truth in us when we meet

Him, understand Him accurately, and remember Him. The One who tells us our future, and gives us a fresh reason for living – and removes all fear of dying. The one who gives us a new birth.

In our heart of hearts, Dadi says, everyone knows there is a time when God comes to humanity's rescue, to offer us a fresh start. This is why we so readily say "Oh God" at times of shock or distress.

It is also true that many feel better off *without* a belief in God. Human beings have developed many conflicting ideas about God, and performed many cruel actions in His name. Moreover, science has so improved material circumstances for many that they are able to enjoy life in the here and now, without worrying about tomorrow. A worthwhile job, a loyal partner, children, grandchildren ... all these can be a source of joy.

The source of pain

If our attitude towards any of the assets in our lives becomes too worldly, however, they can start to seem like burdens rather than joys. It all has to do with whether we stay loving and giving, or become grasping. Eventually, any dependency on people, or possessions, or worldly positions, will become a source of pain and suffering.

A parent who takes the wrong kind of pride in a child's achievements will have their happiness destroyed if that same child becomes severely ill, or unexpectedly fails their exams, for example. Then the child also has a double burden, coping not only with their new circumstances but with the parent's distress as well.

The executive who invests too much of himself in building a thriving company will be devastated by financial loss or ruin, to the point that unless he learns from his mistake, he might never again find the strength to build another enterprise.

The wife or husband who invests too much of him or herself in their spouse will find their world shattered if divorce, or death, takes the partner away.

Does this mean we should not love our children, or work, or partner? Of course not. However, the love has to be free-flowing, not binding, and without expectations from the other. In today's world, the wisdom and capacity to live in this way is rare. Even our bodies will turn against us if we ask too much of them. Everyone grows old, and eventually leaves their "mortal coil"; but if we identify too strongly with the body, we will suffer much more at the time of a decline in health, or death, than if we have learned to live lightly.

Staying free from sorrow

Dadi Janki says:

I was not born with this knowledge, and there have been times when I too have suffered. But I have learned so much! There is a wealth of experience inside me, about staying free from sorrow. We do not have to be concerned about anything.

I do still have one strong desire, and it is why, at 99, I am still in this body. My wish is that as many as possible, in the human family, should receive their own inheritance of peace, love, happiness and power from God. These are the inner resources that enable us to experience a good life, free of negative thoughts towards the self or others.

Happiness is a treasure. It nourishes the soul and gives us energy and enthusiasm in life. When we look for it outside of ourselves, it will always be temporary. We have to learn to create it internally. The way to do that is to create pure feelings within, based on inner truth, love, and trust.

For centuries, science kept its focus on the material world, and left God to the religious-minded. At their best, the religions fought bravely to keep the divine alive in our minds, but it has often been a losing battle. Many people, seduced by the material benefits science brought us, adopted a materialistic view of the world that left little place for spirit.

Today, science is acknowledging that our thoughts and feelings profoundly influence our physical health and well-being, even to the point of affecting the functioning of our genes. Information about the world around us enters us through the senses, but its impact on us depends on our understanding, and our inner state of being. In ignorance, or depression, for example, we will feel ultra-vulnerable to what happens around us. As our knowledge grows about the spiritual principles that underpin the way the world works and we gradually feel more fulfilled, we become progressively better able to cope with adversity.

A great deal of information is available nowadays that can help make life more manageable. Skills such as positive thinking, effective communication, mindfulness, anger management, emotional freedom techniques, and so on, do help millions. People often find, however, that it becomes progressively more difficult to maintain these gains. The surge of enthusiasm that comes with fresh hope often fades over time, as old habits reassert themselves.

The light and love with which Dadi felt flooded as a 19-year-old are stronger in her today, 80 years on, than ever. This book points the way towards what is required for all of us to have this direct, practical experience of the divine.

*Each chapter begins with a few lines translated from classic Indian movie songs of the 1930s to 1950s. When Dada Lekhraj shared teachings with the founding members of the spiritual university, these love songs were played as a prelude, mirroring the love of the soul for the Supreme. The lines are reproduced with permission from a re-mastered collection called *Door Ke Musafir* (Traveller from Afar). To hear the songs, go to www.doorkemusafir.com

Chapter 2

Understanding Soul

I have come with my fortune awakened
I have created a new world for myself

"The biggest treasure I have received in my life is an accurate understanding of who I am," Dadi Janki says. "That includes clear knowledge of who God is, because at this time in history we cannot know ourselves except in relation to God.

"It is this relationship that enables me to stay connected to the transcendent, filled constantly with love and power, and at the same time continue as a human being, performing actions and maintaining relationships with others. Today, in fact, far from being retired, I am in relationship with countless others, both from within the Brahma Kumaris and within the world at large."

A subtle understanding permits this state of being. The English word subtle originally meant "finely woven", and one needs a finely woven mental net to catch the feeling of being a soul. It involves shifting one's sense of identity from forms of self-awareness linked one's body and upbringing, such as male or female, Christian or Jew, Hindu or Moslem, rich or poor, young or old, smart or stupid, in favour of an identity that lies deeper than any of those. Physical identity is gross, and quite easily grasped, but temporary. The subtle dimension of reality is refined, and more elusive, but it has a quality of truth about it that makes it very sweet to experience.

So what is the soul? The Brahma Kumaris community felt immense liberation in the understanding and experience that they were not our bodies of flesh and bone, but beings of subtle light, when they first came together in the 1930s and 1940s. Great spiritual power and wisdom were shining through Brahma Baba and this became a catalyst for instant change among them, lifting them out of their habitual bodily identity (or "body-consciousness") so that they could connect with the divine.

They knew from the experience itself what it meant to be a soul. There was a deep peace amongst them, such that when one day a coach full of BK sisters crashed and overturned, injuring many, rescuers were astounded at their quiet acceptance of the scene. Such detachment from physical pain was possible because they were steeped in the practice of knowing themselves at a deeper level than the body.

The actor is not the role

The understanding they developed as time went on, which is so liberating, is that although mind and matter are deeply connected, the soul is the eternal essence of who we are, distinct from the body, which of course has a temporary existence.

They likened the soul's relationship to the body to that of a driver and his car. Developing an awareness of this kind helps to counter the tendency to over-identify with the body, including the brain – a tendency that underpins many of humanity's current difficulties. We say "my arms", "my legs", "my heart", "my brain" and so on, but who is the "I" in relation to whatever we are referring to as "mine"? It is the conscious agent, the soul.

Another useful metaphor for understanding the soul's relationship with the body is that of an actor, and his costume. The costume fits the role he is playing when he is on the stage. So the role and the costume are inherently related. Like mind and matter, they complement and participate with one another. Nevertheless, they are not the same. When the play is over, the actor takes off his costume and leaves the theatre.

The human body is more complex than an actor's costume in that as long as the soul inhabits it, a process of constant renewal enables it to maintain its form. Life is an immensely dynamic process. When the soul leaves the body, however, the renewal ceases, and the form rapidly disintegrates.

The soul – the actor – then goes on to play another part, for as long as the play we are enacting keeps unfolding.

"Can you see how valuable it is," Dadi says, "to develop this consciousness of our own eternity, even whilst living in a body? It removes so much worry and fear. In fact, I would say that the essence of spirituality is to be completely attentive to sustaining this state of soul-consciousness. I want so much that others should experience this freedom!"

Three worlds

An important step towards being able to do so is to learn about where the soul comes from, and where it will ultimately return. To help with understanding about this, the Brahma Kumaris teach a model called the three worlds.

The physical world is the one familiar to us all, set in space and time. This is where the unique potential that lies within each soul or "seed" finds expression. It is like a theatre, in which we souls are actors, performing our individual roles. This worldly stage, however, is not our home, any more than the theatre is an actor's home.

Our place of origin is a timeless and dimensionless world, which lies beyond the material realm. It is rather like the projection room in a cinema. It holds the information relevant to the entire story of existence, as an unbroken whole.

In this "soul world" beyond the physical universe, all of us reside as dimensionless points, in a state of pure potential, timeless and incorporeal. This is our ultimate home. We are like seeds there.

Between the soul world and the physical world is an intermediate aspect of reality called the subtle region, or region of spiritual light. We can compare this to the light that travels between projector and screen in a cinema. The information about the progress of the movie is present within this light, but it only becomes seen by everyone once captured on the screen.

Within the whole, each soul has its own entire, unique part recorded within it. That uniqueness is never lost, even when we are in the home, away from the theatre of life.

Our parts unfold in a glorious way when we first come on to the stage, because of the purity we bring with us from the home. Love, peace, and joy are intrinsic to the human soul, and at that time, we easily and naturally express those qualities in our relationships and through our actions. We are able to live selflessly, functioning harmoniously as in a beautiful choir, fully aware that we are spiritual beings having a human experience.

Gradually, over time (many lifetimes for some), that awareness diminishes. Original, true self-awareness becomes weaker as the consciousness of the body, and attachment to the physical world we inhabit, grows stronger. Eventually, many forget their divine origin completely and identify only with the body and its roles and relationships. This "fall" into body-consciousness brings suffering, a sense of loss, and a consequent growth in worry, fear, and selfishness. This is because everything at the material level is temporary.

If you recognise that you are a soul, you can live life lightly. You know that you have nothing to lose, materially, because even death is a transition. This recognition and awareness is at the heart of Raja Yoga, the study and practice taught by the Brahma Kumaris.

All the world's a stage

From the beginning, the founding sisters worked with the under-standing that the play in which we are actors is pre-determined, and lasts for just a few thousand years. It occupies a wheel of time, which exists eternally.

There is just this one, scripted play. Although souls contribute to the way it unfolds, the way we choose to play our parts is just as much a part of eternity as any other aspect. It is as though we give a live performance in the theatre of life, but at a deep level, that performance is a part of the unchanging whole.

Between parts, we have a taste of the unlimited, as indicated by the stories of those who have had a near-death experience (NDE), "dying" to this body and then being resuscitated. NDE-ers describe moving through different levels of awareness, from the worldly to the sublime. People who have suffered brain damage sometimes describe the same experience, of going beyond the body to a realm of love and light, where soul identity is still present but the mind feels connected to the whole and can travel wherever it wishes.

When the wheel of time has turned full circle and the play ends, our consciousness leaves both the material and subtle worlds, and we return to our original state of pure potential in the soul world. Because the play is eternal, however, we do not stay off-stage forever. On cue, all the actors return to play their roles, as eternity continues to unfold in its cyclical fashion.

The aim in Raja Yoga is to become so knowledgeable and powerful as to be able to stay in the awareness of the three worlds, and the different experiences appropriate to each, even whilst we continue to play our parts on the stage of the world through these bodies.

Longing for truth

To over-identify with the body and its roles is to compromise your happiness. Changes that take place as your own body ages, or as death approaches, may become a great burden to you. The loss, or threatened loss, of relatives who are important to the way you define yourself and your place in the world become a source of worry and grief. The same may become true of your work or career. Today, many people's lives are plagued in this way by insecurity and fear.

Sometimes, in an effort to ease the pain and fill the hollowness they feel, people drive themselves to extraordinary heights of worldly achievement. They may build a billion-dollar business empire, or reach championship level in sport, or high office in politics or academia. When the motivation comes from this sense of spiritual deficit, however, the achievements usually feel hollow as well, and rarely satisfy. Such driven individuals can damage many others along the way, even a whole society.

Nowadays Dadi Janki travels less, but there was a time when she visited almost every corner of the world. She says that as she did so, she found a widespread longing for a return to truth, and an escape from the sense of isolation caused by body-consciousness.

When unfulfilled, this longing makes us vulnerable, in a variety of ways. Some people keep suffering in their personal relationships, having unrealistic expectations of their partners. Others may be taken in, *en masse*, by charismatic leaders offering religious, political or economic ideologies that seem to offer hope of a better life, but eventually prove disastrous. History offers many examples of how people have mistakenly interpreted a limited sense of purpose and unity, rooted in a negative attitude towards others, as "divine" justification for violent and abusive behaviour.

This is why we need to know very precisely who we are as individuals, and how we can come together again in a way that will avoid these dangers. We have gone wrong so often in the past that there is widespread scepticism of any claims to have found "the truth".

Nevertheless, based on the wisdom that came through Brahma Baba and on her own long lifetime's study and practice, Dadi shares the conviction that only God can sort out this mess, and that we are living in an era when He does so. An under-standing of God is key to success in this endeavour.

Chapter 3

Understanding God

You alone are the stick for the blind
You alone are the light of my life

The Brahma Kumaris began with pure soul experiences so powerful that nothing, and no one, could stop them running to Dada Lekhraj and the movement he started. He showed immense courage in withstanding enormous family and community pressures to shut down the movement. Some of the men who opposed them, angered by the challenge to their power and authority by daughters and wives whom they expected to be submissive, behaved very badly.

Looking back after nearly 80 years, however, it is easy to see how some misunderstandings arose.

It is an ancient belief in India, enshrined in some of the scriptures, that a web of mind-like energy holds together the material world. The idea is finding support at the frontiers of modern physics: see, for example, chapter 18 of *The Black Hole War*, by Leonard Susskind (Back Bay Books, 2008). Over the millenia, however, it gave rise to what the Brahma Kumaris now see as a profound misconception. This is the belief that God is everywhere, even in inanimate objects like pebbles and stones.

In those early days in Hyderabad and Karachi, the founding sisters felt such a strong sense of oneness in the gathering that they used to say that all of them, and especially their beloved Dada Lekhraj, were God. They made no clear distinction between the soul and the Supreme.

The pull they felt towards the gathering was so strong that in the view of some onlookers, the only explanation possible was that Lekhraj was a hypnotist holding sway over vulnerable young women and lonely wives. Fortunately, when independent authorities came to check them out, they saw a reformist group acting according to high spiritual principles and pure motives.

As their study together continued, it became clear to the sisters that although there can be a beautiful sense of union with God when a soul becomes steeped in love for the divine, fully detached from the pull of the body and worldly life, God always remains God, and we remain God's children.

Loving God

Let nothing disturb you
Nothing frighten you,
All things are passing;
Patient endurance
Attains all things.
One whom God possesses
Lacks nothing
For God alone suffices.
– St Teresa of Avila

Dadi Janki asks:

Where and how should I begin, in telling you about loving God? It is difficult enough to convey to others the love you might feel for another human being, since 'beauty is in the eye of the beholder'. With God, too, there have been countless ideas and opinions.

I have learned that the way to be close to God is to have a clean heart, full of good wishes and pure feelings towards others, with no animosity. However, most of us require a catalyst or spur to set us on the road towards recovering such fullness and cleanliness in spirit. Love is definitely the greatest spur, but we also need wisdom, and determination to keep going no matter what obstacles come in the way.

My own initial inspiration was the inner work that Brahma Baba did. Through his practice of soul-consciousness, he maintained high quality thoughts and feelings in the face of all provocation, and gained such stability as to be able to reveal and transmit divine power. That was what drew so many of us towards him. We wanted to give our lives to the task of being able to do the same for others.

It is the opening of this 'third eye', the eye of inner recognition and understanding, which connects us to God. When we simply loved God in a devotional way, taking on board ideas passed down through the centuries, there was a lot of scope for individual interpretation and bias. The world now needs a global renewal of consciousness, and for that we need absolute clarity about who we are, who God is, and what we must now do.

Becoming like God

The idea that God is everywhere is common in the East. It can be seen as an expression of devotional feelings, but it obscures the ability to take power from God. It is true that Nature contains qualities that can remind us of God. There are also subtle mechanisms at work in the physical world that have reminded mystics and others able to access them of deeper realities. The firmament is imbued with divine energy. However, if God is everywhere – in you and me, and in the sun and stars and pebbles and stones – who is going to help us recover our truth?

God is best understood as incorporeal, bodiless, dimensionless. He exists outside space and time. He is the architect, not the building; the artist, not the painting. Just as astronomers and mathematicians theorise that the physical universe originated in what they call a singularity – a dimensionless point – such also is God's form.

As souls, each of us has the same form, a point. Knowledge of this likeness between souls and God enables us to know Him and love Him, and receive power from Him. When we still the mind, draw our conscious energies into a point (which can be envisaged as in the centre of the forehead, behind the eyes), and remember that our home lies beyond this physical world, it is as though a line of connection opens up. In that seed-like awareness, we reconnect to our own highest nature of peace, love, and joy, and know the master Seed. There is a fullness, a contentment, in this deep self-awareness that automatically connects us to the Supreme, as in the Biblical saying "Be still, and know that I am the Lord thy God".

In Raja Yoga the aim is not to merge into God, as some religious traditions aspire to, but rather, to become like God in terms of power and virtue. When we remember that we too are eternal beings, we can feel ourselves filling again with God's qualities of love and peace. We are able to experience ourselves as unlimited love, because this is the highest truth about us.

In the 'soul world', our home beyond time and space, we live with God in a state of pure potential. We are a part of a whole, but a whole part, complete in ourselves. Remembering this original and eternal wholeness of ours, even whilst here in a body, in the physical world, we can 'tune in' to God, and resonate with that highest Source of power.

Lost divinity

The power we receive from God is the power of truth. In everyday life, through body-consciousness, most of us have acquired habits of self-deception. We pursue selfish desires whilst pretending that our actions are for the benefit of others. We hide from our mistakes, gradually killing our conscience, suppressing our highest nature of love and compassion. We justify our anger, dehumanize our enemies, and give reasons and excuses for our weak and selfish behaviour.

To different degrees, all of us have lost our truth because of losing sight of our divinity. We are beings of consciousness; and when our consciousness became over-absorbed in the material world, we forgot that we are souls.

God does not condemn us for this. In His eyes, our state of ignorance is simply how things are, as of today. He has no more reason to criticise us than the sun to criticise the darkness before the dawn, or winter to wish it were spring.

The perfect relationship

Through Brahma Baba's visions, however, the founding members of the spiritual university gained the insight that God is not an entirely neutral observer of this play of existence. God is a living entity, and has a central role within the play. The most significant aspect of His role is to remind us of who we are, and what He is, when ignorance and the suffering it brings are becoming extreme. The call to human beings at this time is to reawaken and restore truth in ourselves through remembering Him, and thereby to restore truth in the world.

The Supreme Soul has to come here, into the play itself, the world of space-time and matter, to perform this task. He comes here, to show us how to take our minds there, above and beyond, to the soul world.

He comes as a Mother and Father, concerned to find His lost children, and take them into His arms in order to refresh and renew them. He comes as a Lover, and each of us is His beloved. He is our Friend, who fills us with the courage, inspiration, faith, patience and strength to keep going on the pilgrimage of spiritual renewal, even when the path is rocky and seems strewn with obstacles.

In fact, he fulfils every relationship of value to us. He is our Teacher, who tells us what happened in the past, and what is about to happen, so that we may understand what has been going on and prepare for what is to come. He is our Guide and Companion, who shows us the practical steps we need to take to get from a world where sorrow and suffering have become widespread, to a land of unalloyed truth.

Dadi Janki says that in the early days of the BK movement, they felt the presence of God among them so intensely that for some, transformation was rapid.

Brahma Baba developed such a natural practice of remaining bodiless that, towards the end of his life, it was as though everything he said and did was on God's behalf. He became the perfect trustee; his mind, body and wealth used only in God's service. He sought no recognition for himself, but taught us to understand that God was working through him to establish the true consciousness that would enable the return of a world of happiness.

Our exposure to this purity of intention was one of the factors that enabled us to feel that we were receiving a new birth. Feeling such happiness, peace and love in ourselves, we no longer saw defects in others, only goodness. We saw each other as souls, children of the Supreme Being. We understood that we had all just come into the physical world to play our parts. This world was now old, filled with dishonesty, falsehood and violence, but it was soon to change.

Chapter 4

Understanding Time

Who has created this game
Who has created all the music
You did all of this alone
Then hid Yourself away

In the understanding of cyclical time, even the part played by God is preordained within the subtle mechanism of the drama. There is power in this way of thinking. It means God is not a capricious, supernatural agent whom we need to fear. God really is peace, and love. He is the Seed of all that is highest in human beings. To know Him and remember Him is to activate the positive blueprints of our own being. By doing this repeatedly, with attention, we restore our own peaceful and loving nature.

The understanding shared by God of a repeating cycle of time is also empowering. It enables us to comprehend how we lost our truth, and why we are now to regain it.

It offers us a story of a humanity that begins its journey through time in a state of perfection, a golden age, where we live in harmony with one another and with the rest of the natural world. Violence and war are unthinkable, because we understand that we are spirit, connected by vibrations of love, and do not identify with the material forms that would otherwise seem to separate us. This paradise is, quite simply, the outward expression of the original blueprint of life, the early "script" of the eternal drama of existence.

A play in four acts

The play is in four acts, of equal duration. It begins with the golden age, remembered in religious traditions as heaven on earth. A silver age follows, in which there are the beginnings of a divided world, but still a strong spiritual awareness.

As matter continues to infiltrate our consciousness, there is radical change. Like a crystal weakened by too many flaws, the oneness of mind that characterises the first half of the cycle suddenly shatters. Physical upheaval, remembered in most ancient cultures as the time of a great flood, accompanies this mental event. From that time onwards, we are in a divided world.

Great prophets and teachers like Abraham, Christ, Buddha and Muhammad uplift millions by reminding them of the deeper realities, and of how to live in ways that honour our higher nature. They become the founders of religions – strong branches of thought within which different sections of humanity recover a sense of belonging and unity.

Overall, however, the loss of spiritual awareness continues throughout the second half of the play. Eventually it reaches the point where divine intervention is needed. This happens through an injection of pure consciousness. God comes to remind all souls that they belong to Him, and to enable them to leave their bodies and return home to the soul world, so that the cycle may begin anew.

This is God's main role, and why so many remember Him, consciously or unconsciously, as their ultimate Saviour. He recreates both the spiritual awareness that will take us home, and the consciousness that restores heaven on earth.

Another aspect of the power and beauty of this understanding is that it gives a feeling of eternity, whilst accommodating the present. Many do understand that by living in the present moment, we can align ourselves better with life's flow than if we cling on to past events, or worry about the future. However, it may not be possible to stay constantly "in the now", if you are to continue to engage in life in today's far-from-perfect world. Knowledge of where we stand today in relation to the overall cycle of time helps with self-understanding, and with understanding others. It enables us to accept ourselves as the flawed beings we are, whilst not losing sight of what we were originally, and are to become.

Visions in Varanasi

The knowledge of the cycle came to Brahma Baba in the early 1930s. He was staying at a friend's house in Varanasi, India's oldest city, when he found himself repeatedly drawing circles on a wall. Graphic visions that he experienced at the same time included apocalyptic scenes of death and destruction, followed by a vision of stars gently descending to earth and where they landed, perfect human beings – deities – springing up like flowers.

The body of teachings that developed over the following years has become the basis of renewal in the lives of many. It includes the understanding that once here on the stage of the physical world, human souls take rebirth until the end of the cycle, when all return home together. For most of the cycle, the population constantly increases, as more and more "actors" join the stage.

Dadi Janki says that Brahma Baba found great self-respect and joy in anticipating the time when his highest potential would be made actual. He realised also that successive births had brought a gradual loss in his ability to live by that highest truth. Now his aim was to renew himself fully through remembrance of God, and the golden age to come.

Moreover, he was inviting us to do the same! We too could become masters of the age of truth by letting go of our old natures and surrendering ourselves to the loving embrace of the spiritual Father.

Those were joyful days. We were lost in spiritual love. We felt that heaven was imminent. In fact, we were so deeply in love that for some it was as if we were already in heaven. The old world meant nothing to us. With our minds we were with the Father, the Highest-on-High, and nothing else mattered. There was great power in this awareness, helping us to put the past behind us and move towards a fresh state of being.

Lifelong learning

As the years passed, we understood that God was not here just for us, but for the whole of humanity, and preparing us for lives of service. We realised that human beings everywhere are suffering because of the loss of awareness of soul. Just as we were finding happiness and freedom through the knowledge shared with us by the Supreme, we must contribute to the task of enabling others to do the same.

Despite our joy at feeling we had found God, we learned that the job of self-renewal requires dedicated time and attention over a long period. Old habits die hard, and most of us would be continuing to learn throughout our lives. Even today, I consider myself a Godly student. Every day brings fresh opportunities to increase in spiritual capacity and power.

I have seen thousands choose to lead lives of service, in great simplicity, in India and abroad. Hundreds of thousands more are pursuing the goal of self- and world-renewal in everyday circumstances. The fullness of heart that comes from accurate remembrance of God transforms relationships with family members and work colleagues.

When the inner journey, the inner transformation, is suffi-ciently central in your life and awareness, what happens outside of you becomes a testing ground that helps you move forward. External relationships and events show you how far you have come in maintaining stability and love, and where there is room for improvement. Progress brings great happiness; setbacks become a spur to greater learning. This makes for a wonderful life.

The next section of this book describes how the understandings that have underpinned and informed most of Dadi Janki's life provide a way of escaping from the traps that our body-consciousness created, so that we can follow her example in becoming free.

Part 2: Life

"A human being is part of a whole, called by us the 'Universe' — a part limited in time and space. He experiences himself, his thoughts, and feelings, as something separated from the rest — a kind of optical delusion of his consciousness. This delusion is a kind of prison for us, restricting us to our personal desires and to affection for a few persons nearest us. Our task must be to free ourselves from this prison by widening our circles of compassion to embrace all living creatures and the whole of nature in its beauty."

– Albert Einstein

Chapter 5

Power of Truth

Look at your face in the mirror, O man
See how much charity and how much sin
You have done in your life

The divine love and wisdom Dadi Janki and many others received through Brahma Baba set their lives on a fresh course. It was as though they had taken a new birth.

They understood the knowledge and experience to have come from God, but it was down to each one of them to work with it and put it into practice in such a way that it became not just a short-term comfort, or future aspiration, but a power that could really inform their lives.

Dadi says that in order to achieve this, she pays great attention to using her *intellect* to keep her heart happy, her mind on track, her brain cool, and her nature simple.

Over the years, this has brought an inner strength that enables me to hold my peace, and a loving attitude, no matter what happens externally. This is good for me, especially now my body is old, because it minimizes the energy I have to spend in my relationships and connections with others – nothing goes to waste. It is also good for others, because they receive a share, vibrationally, of the peace and love that are in me when they come into my connection. On top of that, the more cool and loving we are, as opposed to hot and bothered, the more clearly we can see how best to act.

Most animals respond to life events instinctively. Their instincts tend not to vary anything like as much as human beings' do, although as farmers and pet owners know, they certainly have their individuality. Humans are different in that the quality of our actions changes greatly over time. Although all souls share love, peace and joy as our original nature, our journey through time compromises our ability to express those qualities, until eventually, body-consciousness dominates our awareness.

Recognising toxic beliefs

Body-consciousness means much more than being conscious of our bodies. It is shorthand for a whole package of conditioned responses to people and circumstances, stemming from an over-identification with the physical aspects of life and loss of awareness of soul.

Body-consciousness is the enemy of pure love, peace and joy. The belief that we are bodies has toxic consequences. It acts as a gateway to worry, fear, and sorrow. We worry that something bad will happen to us. We become afraid if it looks as if it might happen; and if it does happen, we fill with sorrow.

For example, you may worry intensely about the health of your body, or the security of your job, or that your partner may leave you, because you have lost sight of the fact that all of those factors are external to you, the soul. The worry becomes a pattern, deepening your insecurity, until it becomes fear. Fear blocks your ability to love, and take proper care. Therefore in time your body, work and relationships all start to deteriorate because of your thinking, rather than because of the circum-stances themselves.

It becomes clear that the suffering is self-induced when we look at how differently individuals respond to life challenges. One person's obstacle can be a life-enhancing take-off point for another. Loss of a job or partner may be devastating to one individual and the start of a new life for someone else.

Internal sources of security

A key to how we respond is the extent to which we have internalised a sense of self-respect. Someone who has grown up with a lot of love is more likely to sail smoothly through setbacks than someone who feels permanently hungry for love. For the latter, a loss or threatened loss can bring an unbearable sense of doom, leading to mental breakdown or some other health crisis.

It is not just a matter of whether our parents or siblings loved us, however. Our dispositions vary greatly. One child may bring sunshine into a home, while another seems permanently under a shadow. Spiritual understanding tells us that souls carry different predispositions, according to their past actions. A predominance of positive actions in one birth is likely to give rise to favourable circumstances, including a sunny disposition, in the next – and vice versa.

The beauty of Raja Yoga is that through God's love and wisdom, we develop the power to change negative aspects of our life trajectory into positive. We learn that our gradual decline into body-consciousness caused us to lose sight of our inner power, thus weakening us and making us vulnerable to hurt. We discover that the remedy is to regain true self-respect through awareness of the soul in relation to the Supreme.

We have to make an effort to keep the heart clean. That means keeping it filled with God's mercy, truth, and love, and not leaving space for negative feelings such as unhappiness or loneliness, jealousy or criticism. Then body, mind and words all serve well, and our happiness multiplies.

In contrast, those who only work through their head eventually take sorrow into their heart. The neglected heart becomes hungry for love and respect, making it vulnerable to the attitudes and behaviour of others, so that it too easily comes into all kinds of feeling.

Dadi Janki says:

> Everything starts with the heart. It takes in and harbours feelings, which shape our attitude and vision towards others. My aim is to experience truth in the heart, constantly filling with love and wisdom and the colour of God's company. This elevated relationship enables the yoga of the intellect to become powerful, such that God can draw the soul upwards, and the soul can draw on His love at any time. Then whoever even remembers me only sees me as belonging to One. Such yoga is the basis of the establishment of the new world.

Capacity for conscious change

I have mentioned that whereas most animals act according to a relatively fixed blueprint, the quality of human actions changes along with changes of awareness. Fortunately, we also differ from animals in that we have the capacity to become self-aware and consciously to bring about improvements in our attitudes and in the ways we see the world.

The intellect, restored to strength through relationship with God, is the tool that makes this possible. It is useful to distinguish the intellect from the mind, though in a state of truth, both work harmoniously together. According to whatever is foremost in the mind, so we experience the world. The mind presents our conscious awareness with thoughts and feelings. Based on which thoughts and feelings are coming to the fore, so our actions follow.

Body-consciousness compromises and eventually corrupts our original, positive nature. It takes over the mind, as bodily appetites, ambitions and desires dominate our thinking. Selfish and destructive behaviour increases. To begin with, the intellect may try to restrain these negative impulses. It tells us that they are wrong, and not in accordance with our true nature. The conscience bites. Perhaps we find the strength to resist the temptation to act in a way that would contravene our humanity.

However, as ignorance of our true nature increases, and body-consciousness takes more of a hold, the conscience slowly dies. It is as if the intellect turns to stone. It is generally "old souls", who have taken many births, who are subject to this loss of truth, though it can also happen within the course of a single lifetime.

The good news, Dadi Janki says, is that the process is reversible!

I know, because I have done it myself, as well as seeing many others do the same. Although I always longed for truth, I have not always had the strength to live in accordance with my highest nature. Now, my lifelong effort has brought me to that place of truth where my heart, mind, intellect and nature have become like the Father's, complete with happiness and peace, asking nothing, receiving constantly from God, and sharing that happiness with others.

Need for courage

It is easy, but it does require courage. One reason for this is that as you climb higher, so the falls, when they come, are steeper. You need patience, and humility. Above all, you need to want to restore truth in yourself with all your heart.

It is when both intellect and mind have absorbed and can work with the knowledge of who I am, as a child of God, that the soul regains truth. The intellect tells the mind and heart: "Remember that Supreme Father, in the home beyond. Feel the joy of knowing that you belong to that One. Understand that you are a soul, whose original nature is like the Father's, wise, detached and loving. Know that you came from that home, in common with all other souls, and will return there soon."

When the mind has recognised the beauty of the relationship with God, it easily remembers the experience of being at one with the Supreme and keeps returning to that memory. This is Raja Yoga. It fills the soul with the power of truth.

At first the experience may only come in meditation, when we sit specially to remember. As we grow stronger, we become able to stay connected to the One whilst in action. It is as though the Supreme becomes our Companion, helping us to overcome our negative predispositions and emerge our highest potential. Then it feels as if He is doing everything. We become genuinely and lastingly free.

Whatever is in our awareness will emerge in our attitude towards people and circumstances, and consequently in our words and actions. Painful or unpleasant memories that linger on in our awareness act like a straightjacket, restraining us from fulfilling our potential in life. When the past has infiltrated our awareness deeply, we may sink into a depressive state. We may realise we should not be turning over those old memories, but they have a hold on us that may be difficult to shake off.

We need to bring the light of understanding on to these memories, so we can move on. That becomes possible, Dadi says, "when we listen to God with a true heart, and keep the mirror of the mind clean. The intellect does this job. An active and loving intellect keeps listening to the story God tells us, of how we changed from beautiful to ugly and are now becoming beautiful again. Keeping that image of inner beauty in mind, we see how to remove the dirt left by past experiences, and how to prevent the messy scenes of today's external world from entering and influencing us."

Kind to the mind

This ability to look at the self objectively increases as we realise the value of finding peace and strength through accessing divine love and wisdom, and through following divine directions. As the intellect inculcates truth and becomes clean and pure, it starts to see clearly again – and then the mind becomes peaceful. The intellect learns to be kind to the mind, not suppressing it but keeping it in order with love and understanding, and thereby restoring it to its natural beauty and purity.

In an easy, non-violent way, the heart becomes able to let go of wanting this and that. We live in these bodies, maintaining family and other relationships, but the more we become aware that we are souls, the more carefree we remain.

In soul-consciousness, we look out at the world through these eyes with love and detachment. Our perception results from what we are inside, not from what is outside. As we accumulate this internal power of truth, our actions as well as vision become positive, giving happiness to others and removing their sorrow.

When we let ourselves become subservient to nature or other people, we cannot remain happy. Such subservience upsets the soul. When we keep the intellect linked with the One, we achieve mastery: the mind stays detached and peaceful, the heart remains full of love, the brain and sense organs become cool and the body experiences rest. We go beyond the "taste" of former yearnings.

Dadi Janki says:

We need to maintain the awareness that the Supreme Soul really is our Father, and that He is there to give us this power. He is giving, and our part is to receive. God's love and wisdom flows freely when we let Him be our all; when we feel from the heart that "Mine is One and none other." We are then able to free ourselves further from desires, from attraction, and from external influence. Whatever is going on outside of us – praise or defamation, victory or defeat – we remain unshakeable. This is to be in a state of truth.

Even if something from outside enters the heart and causes

pain, affecting the mind, the intellect knows what to do: it tells the heart to be quiet, and with love, removes the thorn. Otherwise, when something happens and we keep remembering it, we will experience sorrow, and others will feel that too.

Habit of taking sorrow

To give and take sorrow is a type of illness. It is a habit. It makes us over-sensitive and delicate, and insensitive to the hurt we may cause others. Ultimately, there are no valid excuses for this, though the ego may offer a lot of reasons and explanations.

Remain aware that everyone has their own part in this world play, and that only our good wishes and pure feelings can help improve a situation. No amount of complaining, or suffering, on our part is of any use. Repeatedly thinking about others brings down our stage of consciousness, and allowing ourselves to become upset inevitably causes sorrow to others as well.

When we remember this, we will not let ourselves become unhappy, even by mistake, but keep smiling. Otherwise, the habit of taking sorrow will never leave us, and we will continue to experience sorrow even from little things, as if being constantly pricked by a pin. It might be nothing at all, but our thinking makes it into something. This is no way to live!

When our heart is true to God, it can be strong. That is, neither overly soft – delicate and fragile – nor hardened inside and consequently hard on others. The heart becomes truly merciful. It is not afraid to speak clearly to others, because its motive is love. To be merciful towards someone does not mean letting him or her do as they wish, regardless. It means to be able to speak in such a loving way that they feel this good intention, and are able to understand and accept. In contrast, if we speak from a place of ego, no one will listen.

To see each other with feelings of respect and love brings great happiness, and generates energy. Love and truthfulness help others to change themselves, and let go of negative tendencies. If we have the thought that someone will never change, and that to give up on them is a safer or more sensible option, that is our own ego speaking. To be merciful means always remembering only that which is good and beneficial, and never letting go of giving love.

Connection between love and peace

There is a connection between love and peace. For as long as the heart is looking for love, the mind cannot be peaceful. All over the world, there is a shortage of love, and peace has been broken into pieces. Everyone, young and old, wants love. Both sick and healthy people want love. Love can remove sickness, and help us forget our illness. However, if we remember a negative situation, we feel sorrow in the heart.

Love is a gift from the Supreme Being, which we keep in the heart. The Supreme also brings light, which enables us to learn to love everything from the heart. Love is natural. Whilst the soul is in the body, there is the love of relationships with people; but when we go beyond the body, we receive such pure and unlimited love from the Supreme as to finish all our defects and weaknesses. As much as we recognise Him from the heart, we receive light and might from Him, and then through the intellect we can feel and understand the value of His company and power.

In soul-consciousness, everything can be resolved. The intellect looks inwards, and upwards, rather than pointing the finger outwards. Otherwise, the mind goes in so many places: towards the body, relationships, money, food, ambitions, and so on. This is why God has told us to focus on Him alone, in order to develop divine virtues, and *then* bring them into our practical lives. Only in this is there benefit.

We are souls, in bodies, and we have to bring into order our eyes, ears, mouth, nose, and so on, so that rather than allow them to pull us here and there, we reclaim our sovereignty. If we are not truthful, we cannot be loving, nor experience peace and happiness. God gives true knowledge, and makes us true.

We do not lose our individuality as God restores truth inside us, but become simple and carefree, transparent and uncomplicated. This reality brings royalty, and a wonderful state of humility. Our old, limited desires, which made us restless and ego-driven, fall away. When we are loyal and true to our Beloved in this way, keeping Him as our Companion, our faces become bright and smiling, and we feel at one with others. Our lives become beacons of light.

Chapter 6

Power of Purity

Even after the moon ceases to exist
The stars cease to exist
I will remain forever Yours

There is an old saying in English, "Cleanliness is next to Godliness". This does not refer only to physical cleanliness. The deeper meaning is that in order to keep the heart connected to God, and the intellect's line of understanding clear, constant vigilance is required to prevent a build-up of the "dust" of body-consciousness.

Dust and dirt come in many forms, and some are much bigger enemies of truth than others.

One area in which the teachings of the Brahma Kumaris have produced a big challenge to conventional morality is that of sexual lust. Brahma Baba used to call it the greatest enemy. It does not just create a superficial body-consciousness. It is like poison for the soul.

The reason is that it is a great pretender. It pretends to be an expression of love, of coming out of the narrow prison of the self and reaching out towards another. In addition, through its very intensity, it can give a brief taste of bliss, of freedom from everyday worries. This is why it is so important to so many. In a dry world, which has forgotten the bliss of deep soul-awareness, the fulfilment of sexual desire brings momentary respite.

The satisfaction offered by lust is illusory, however. Its basis is not true freedom, but rather, a process of physical arousal and release that readily becomes addictive rather than liberating.

Dying alive

I have described how when people "die" clinically, only to be resuscitated some time later, they sometimes recall having moved into a state of bliss, linked to a heightened awareness, during the period when body and brain ceased to function. These Near-Death Experiences include a feeling of divine connection so powerful that on their return the resuscitated individuals often change their lives dramatically. They want to live less for themselves, and instead find joy in serving and coming close to others.

The spiritual practices that have formed the basis of Dadi Janki's life facilitate a similar state of consciousness. In fact, the BKs sometimes describe the aim of this life as "dying alive". The bliss that accompanies successful yoga is so great as to enable those who experience it to let go easily of limited, worldly pleasures, and instead to want to give their lives in service to others.

Sex lust does the opposite. Just think how many lives the sex drive has ruined! Sexual violence, including rape, and sexual abuse of children and teenage girls blight the lives of millions, often taking place within the family and going unreported, but leaving victims mentally scarred for life. Men suffer as well: sex outside marriage wrecks countless relationships, and destroys careers. Addiction to sex, especially in the age of internet pornography, has caused growing numbers of men to lose their jobs, families, friends, and self-respect.

Perhaps worst of all, when sex plays too big a part in our thinking, it gives rise to damaging ways of relating to one another. Sexuality often leads to controlling patterns of thought and behaviour. The quest for control can degenerate into extremes of selfish and inhumane behaviour, cutting its victims off not only from other people, but from the care and compassion intrinsic to the soul.

In this way, the positive impulses behind "making love" can

transform into an addictive lust, which readily becomes demanding, and often violent. In the lives of many, sex has become tyrannical, draining them of their humanity rather than promoting love and connectedness.

These are among the reasons why from the start of the spiritual university, Brahma Baba encouraged celibacy, even within marriage. At this crucial time in history, if Raja Yogis were to renew themselves through relationship with the One above, they needed to change the way they related to human beings.

Sublimation not suppression

The idea that abstention from sex can aid communication with the divine is not new. Hinduism, Buddhism, and ancient Greek thought have seen celibacy as an empowering option. The Roman Catholic Church still considers it an essential vow for the priesthood, though sex scandals involving priests and nuns have led to calls for a change of policy.

If the sex drive is suppressed, rather than sublimated, it can cause havoc. However, when we learn how to connect accurately with the divine, the bliss of this relationship and the strengths to which it gives rise diminish the power of the sex drive. The Dutch philosopher Spinoza (1632-77) wrote: "We do not find joy in virtue because we control our lusts: but, contrariwise, because we find joy in virtue we are able to control our lusts."

Does this mean you cannot live a virtuous life unless you are celibate? Not at all. Nor does it mean that someone who practises celibacy is more virtuous than someone who does not.

Nevertheless, experience says that in today's world sex lust is the root of much wrongdoing and unhappiness. It is a great enemy of the soul's intrinsic qualities of love, peace and bliss. The choice to remain celibate, or at least to move in that direction, can be one of the most important steps a person makes in bringing God into their life.

Attitude of being a trustee

Nowadays people look to physical intimacy to overcome boredom and loneliness, but once relationships entangle us, it becomes harder to connect with God. Brahma Baba had children and grandchildren but showed that by fulfilling his responsibilities towards them with an attitude of being a trustee, rather than with a sense of ownership, he could keep his mind and intellect free to keep connecting with the Supreme. He dropped any sense of dependency on people or facilities, and this enabled him to remain fully aware of what he needed to do in order to be able to fulfil an unlimited role in service of the world.

Such freedom requires the determined thought, or realisation, that you wish to break all the bondages that limit your happiness. This is the ultimate purity. It is not necessary to think that there will always be a mixture of happiness and sorrow in your life. That in itself is a limiting belief. The goal of Raja Yoga is to be able to stabilise the self in all circumstances, so as not to experience sorrow.

Dadi Janki says:

It is a matter of the heart. God simply wants us to give Him our heart. When we can say from the heart that we are His, and He is ours, there is such a powerful feeling of belonging that all external dependencies finish. We become free from animosity. Nothing negative remains. We become patient, humble, and sweet. There is no feeling of being isolated or lonely. Then we use our energies well, and from having been feeling empty and confused, we find that everything in life becomes right.

Ordinary and egotistical thoughts decrease our purity. Some have ego of their spiritual effort! Others take pride in the beauty or strength of their body, or greatness of their position, or have arrogance about the charitable actions they perform.

When we allow such thought patterns to take hold within ourselves, God becomes distant.

Even the desire to give happiness to others, or the belief that it is our responsibility to do so, can be a subtle form of dependency or bondage. No matter how much we try, they will never be satisfied if our actions arise through relationship based on the body. The sign that bondage is present is that we will feel sad or insulted when we find we cannot meet the needs of the other. If the relationship breaks down, there will be a lot of sorrow.

It is true that the desire to please others has its origins in our humanity, which makes it hard to recognise as a bondage. However, when this desire emerges from an inner space of body-consciousness, it has selfishness hidden within it.

When we are spiritually full, through knowing and experiencing the self as a child of God, our giving is free-flowing and unconditional. It is as if God gives through us.

If we are to experience complete freedom, we must sit in silence, look within ourselves very deeply, and see how our consciousness should be in order that our actions do not bind us. For as long as subtle ego remains, it will affect everything we do, and we will keep feeling unappreciated or disregarded. We have to understand that our own thinking causes us sorrow, not the behaviour of others.

Care with thoughts and feelings

When we know that a particular food is bad for our health, we avoid it. Similarly, we must be very careful with our thoughts and feelings. Body-consciousness gives rise to incessant desires. It makes us subject to vices such as lust, ego, greed, attachment, and anger, which drain us of strength and destroy our integrity. When negative thoughts are active within the mind, they leave a residue of worry or pain that is like rubbish. Civilised people put their rubbish in a bin! They do not allow it to collect inside their house.

By staying connected to the Divine, I have made myself free of bondage to the customs and systems of our materialistic, body-conscious world that purport to bring benefit, but which actually produce sorrow. A life like this automatically brings happiness to others, as well as to me. When they see how much I care for staying in yoga, and feel the spiritual love that flows towards them because of this divine connection, they feel uplifted and become inspired to make the connection for themselves.

There is no nourishment like happiness. It is a superfood. Devotees remember God as the Remover of Sorrow and Bestower of Happiness, and we can become the same, but we have to remain clean inside to experience this joy continuously. With simplicity in our lives, we can keep drinking the nectar that God gives. Then anything else will seem like poison. The vices brought corruption, violence, sorrow and peacelessness to the world. Purity brings peace, and peace leads to love, and love brings happiness.

Everything in God's hands

What we searched for outside of ourselves, we have now found inside. Once we develop a taste for sitting in silence to drink this nectar, that taste pulls repeatedly. The heart draws us naturally inwards, and we experience a state of introversion. With God in our heart, the space there is occupied and people and situations cannot enter. The intellect becomes stable, unshakeable and immoveable. We feel powerful. Then whatever happens, we will not fluctuate but will remain the observer of the passing scenes. Life brings examinations, but with determination and faith we pass easily.

When we change ourselves, others will change too, but we do not need to worry about other people. Why intrude into their affairs? We do not even need to think about what should happen, according to our own ideas. Everything is in God's hands. It is all a game! The journey of life is a long one and we should enjoy it.

Nevertheless, the world needs people who can sit quietly in a state of peace. When we remain contented, holding God's hand, finishing everything old and limited in us, He makes us do the right things. Then others will be contented with us. When we stay light and free, it is as if we are available to God so that through us, He can get done whatever needs to be done. He will also make us do what is needed for our own benefit. This is the power and beauty of purity.

Let go of thoughts such as 'I'll try' or 'I don't know …' Such thoughts indicate that the heart is not honest, so that you are holding on to confusion and uncertainty. Just take that step of faith, and give your hand to God. One who resolves to stay in God's remembrance can finish the weaknesses of others.

Pure awareness

When I remember God, the feeling is that whatever has happened up to now merges in the mists of time. It has no hold on me. I am present, and fearless. It is as if I sit in God's eyes, and see the whole world as He does, with detachment and love. Everything – past, present, and future – is included in this pure awareness. Lost in this experience, I know that all is well. If I come into the consciousness of problems or situations, God is no longer there.

This Supreme Father is so real, so sweet, and so lovely. When I belong to Him, and keep Him with me, I receive a joy greater than anything the physical world can offer me. The sustenance we receive from God's spiritual love replaces physical love, and gives rise to a great inheritance. It is nothing less than salvation – the restoration of truth inside.

For us to become worthy, effort must come from deep within the heart. It cannot be superficial. The Father's love requires us to keep mind and intellect completely free. We cannot continue with old habits, of losing ourselves in other people, or becoming busy in action. This is a very high study, which entails never remembering anything old or from the past, even from yesterday.

We need to be very conscious of where our mind and intellect are going, because thoughts run as in a stream. What we remember at any one time brings many other thoughts or memories of a similar kind in its wake. For example, if we remember something wasteful or negative, a stream of other connected thoughts and feelings will follow, depleting us of spiritual energy. When we remember God, thoughts connected to the experience of who God is and what He does for us uplift us, and bring benefit in a host of ways.

Creating happiness and strength inside

Dadi emphasises that it is necessary to make time for yoga: to sit in solitude, go deep inside, and recognise and experience the soul and the Supreme.

Words do not easily explain God's love. In fact, we do not even have to think about it too much, or we will not be able to experience it. To understand its depth and quality, we need to move into the experience: "I am a soul, detached from the body and worldly relationships. The One whom the whole world wishes to know is mine. God is getting His work done through me."

We still think and act, but our thoughts are elevated and we act with the awareness that God is doing everything, so that no subtle feeling of arrogance comes. Arrogance prevents us from being forgiving, and gets in the way of compassion.

When we remember the Purifier Father, we become pure. When our thoughts are pure, nothing can be an obstacle in our progress towards reaching the destination of truth. Resolve to have pure and positive thoughts for all! This is a beautiful vow.

Every soul is God's child. The effort we have to make in order to achieve this is constantly to create happiness and strength inside ourselves, by using everything we have – thoughts, time, and energy – in a loving way, and not to keep anything else in our attention. Love is the basis of success.

Without introversion, we cannot do anything worthwhile. With it, the heart becomes full and the intellect concentrated. Remember God from your heart, and you will not remember anything else. Then such power builds inside the soul as to enable us to become part of a new consciousness for a new world. We are sitting in an old home, but our work is to build the new. Eventually, the whole world will cooperate in this task.

There is so much attainment in knowing God, and now is the time to experience this. Ascend, and you taste the sweetness of love. The attainment is so great as to be useful to us for all time.

Kiss introversion! One who is introverted remains happy, and gives happiness. Purity is wonderful. We are on a pilgrimage of life, and time will not stop for anyone. Living or dying, we continue to understand, experience, and enjoy. If we remain happy now, our death will be a good one. When life has been lived well, death becomes easy.

Chapter 7

Power of Positivity

Don't forget the days of your childhood
The path of life is long
Let's travel together while singing and laughing
Let's build a palace in a faraway land
And place a light of love there

In ordinary conditions, and everyday consciousness, things exist independently in relation to each other. An atom is an atom, a table is a table, and a person is a person. Ancient wisdom as well as modern physics, however, tell us that objects are not as separate as they appear, but exist instead within subtle fields that ultimately link the entire universe in an unbroken whole.

Traditional religious and mystical teachings point towards an interconnectedness between people, in particular, which we neglect or ignore at our peril. If we harm others by cheating or stealing from them, or even by thinking negatively towards them, we are at the same time harming ourselves. Failure to recognise this spiritual law due to body-consciousness is one of the reasons why life has become so difficult for many.

In Christianity, a widely used version of *The Lord's Prayer* includes the line: "Forgive us our trespasses, as we forgive them that trespass against us." The word "trespass" means a sin or wrong action in this context, but in modern English, most people would be more familiar with it as meaning to enter someone's land unlawfully. This gives us an insight into the nature of wrong action. Sins are not sins just because someone says so. They are actions that cause loss or hurt when we intrude or "trespass" on another person's space – and this can be mental as well as physical. When we think of sin in this way, it becomes much clearer that it can involve subtle forms of intrusion to which many have become blind.

Dwelling on or gossiping about other people's weaknesses is a common "trespass" of this kind. In themselves, critical thoughts interfere with our ability to be with God. They do not allow us to remain tuned to the divine. Consequently, when we see others with critical vision, we waste time and suffer immediate loss ourselves.

The loss goes deeper than that, however. Because of the subtle interconnections that link us all, a persistently negative attitude towards another is likely to reach them and affect them adversely. It is like a trespass on their mental space, causing them an unwanted loss of subtle energy. Although the effect may not enter their conscious awareness, it is still there. Your relationship with them will suffer and at some point, you are likely to feel the consequences of your intrusion.

You have created what some eastern traditions call a "karmic account" with the person. It is as though you have made an unauthorized withdrawal from their spiritual bank account. The record of what you have done is there and eventually you will have to repay the debt.

This might seem a small matter, but if you fail to realise what you are doing, repeated withdrawals of this kind can wreck a relationship. It is one tragic consequence of the splintered view of life and reality caused by body-consciousness.

Importance of forgiveness

As the Lord's Prayer indicates, forgiveness plays a part in settling these spiritual debts, and in helping to prevent new ones from being established. Forgiveness provides great protection for the self, as well as helping others. It ends vicious cycles of action and reaction. This is why we instinctively admire the example of great leaders such as India's Gandhiji, and South Africa's Nelson Mandela. Through maintaining a positive attitude towards people who had been their oppressors, they worked miracles.

Gandhi and Mandela both worked hard to gain the strength of mind and purpose that allowed them to achieve their objectives, at least in part.

Dadi Janki says:

Imagine the work God has to do, to fulfil the objectives he made known through Brahma Baba's visions, of enabling the return to a world of universal peace! He gets this task done through us human beings. It helps in our spiritual efforts to realise that every drop of improvement we bring to the world through positive choices in our thoughts and feelings is a contribution to this end.

There is a famous image of three wise monkeys, who represent the principle of "see no evil, hear no evil, speak no evil". Sometimes there is a fourth monkey, symbolizing "do no evil". I like also to add that we should think no evil. However, how can we protect ourselves against evil if we do not see it? Will it not simply overwhelm us?

The secret is to "see but not see". Spiritual knowledge allows us to see negativity clearly, and at the same time to maintain a positive vision towards the person. Then we will not feel a need to keep anyone's defects in our heart or mind, let alone spread negativity by speaking about them to others.

We tend to dwell on defects in others when we have not yet done the work of facing up to similar defects in ourselves. When we are free of this reactivity, we will not shy away from quietly putting things right, communicating easily and openly but without going into a lot of expansion.

When I first joined the spiritual community in Karachi, Brahma Baba assigned me to look after more than 40 children in a building called "Baby Bhawan". Their mothers were delighted, because it allowed them to be free. If the children made a mistake, I would say, "OK, today there will be nothing to eat." They would protest, and I would forgive them, telling them not to make that mistake again. They became very well behaved!

Focus on original goodness

At the heart of BK teachings lies the understanding that all souls share God's qualities of love, peace and joy as their original nature, and that this positive charge in the "battery" of the soul becomes run down over time. With this understanding, when evil confronts us, we can focus on the original goodness that is also there in the soul. This eases the other person's negativity. It also protects us. It is like a light that keeps the darkness at bay. If, instead, we become angry or upset, the problem increases all round. A Japanese saying puts it succinctly: "When evil is fought with evil, only evil can win".

Some people, however, have become so lacking in self-respect that they are like black holes, drawing in light and letting out almost nothing in return. We have to be careful not to allow our relationship with another to drain us in this way. Their "trespasses" towards us, especially when unrecognised, may eat away at our own inner strength and leave the soul depleted. Such weakness then makes us even more vulnerable to negative influence, and a vicious circle comes into play. That is when we will be most in danger of reacting, perhaps explosively, and with long-lasting consequences.

Dadi says that when she shares such teachings,

People sometimes say to me, "You don't know what this person is like." I ask them, "Do you think I have lived alone all my life?" I have lived with all kinds. We have to understand that unless we learn how to stay together harmoniously, sorrow will continue to afflict us.

How can we find the strength to stay positive in the face of the many provocations we may meet in the course of a day – or indeed, of a lifetime?

As well as using wisdom and understanding to ensure that we do not cause sorrow to others, we need to know how not to cause sorrow to the self. This is where a true relationship with God is so vital. God's vision towards His human family is unremittingly positive. God is wonderful! When we have His company, nothing else is a big deal. No matter what weaknesses may have penetrated the soul, the Almighty knows that those are not the true self.

Moreover, from His vantage point beyond the material world, He sees the entire play and knows that everything within it has its own purpose and place within the whole. God is the Master of the Unlimited. When I see Him, I also hold the unlimited global family in my awareness. God's vision is of unending love, and when we "go inside" ourselves and keep Him with us, we enjoy the same. This strength creates an energy field around us, which is extremely protective against negative influences. Unpleasant scenes will come, but we will quickly be able to forget them and move on.

At the same time, the positive energy flows out from us and is of genuine help to others. We are able to accept them as they are. We see their strengths rather than dwell on their weaknesses. Being immune to their negativity, we will neither get angry with them, nor feel we have to avoid them. Nor will we feel responsible for them! They have their own parts to play.

Key to life of greatness

As we remain focused on keeping our own inner light burning brightly, this positive spiritual energy will definitely help others. We will not feel we have done anything, however. It is the divine light, not us, that serves. In soul-consciousness, we develop the feeling of becoming instrumental in helping God to restore strength to souls. We cannot do this ourselves.

Nevertheless, in time, such pure feelings towards others automatically bring blessings from them back to us, furthering our own self-confidence and self-respect as well as our value to others. We may not be consciously aware of these blessings, but they will be there; just as surely as we will feel pulled down, eventually, by the ill feelings of those we have wronged.

In these few words, you have the key to a life of greatness. Do not feel that you cannot do it. It is easy, because it is natural. It just takes recognition of who we are, as souls, and of the many beautiful things inside us; love for the One to whom we belong; and determination to honour that Supreme Parent by becoming more and more like Him in our own thoughts, words and actions.

Powerful thoughts are pure, peaceful, elevated and deter-mined. They make others peaceful as well. Weak and wasteful thoughts bring us down. They lower our spirits and diminish our well-being. In the same way, we should be careful not to cause waste thoughts in others, either, by being stubborn or argumentative. If someone does not accept what we say, we should stay light – it does not matter. Do not be upset with anyone, and let no one be upset with us. Everything will be good, because God Himself is with us. Only allow inside what God gives.

God taught me to be honest and truthful, and sustained me with love and truth. Go into the depth of love and truth – seek them from your heart. There is nothing else.

Chapter 8

Power of Honesty

The battle between the weak and the strong
This is the story of the candle and the storm

In physical terms, scientists usually define energy as the capacity of a system to do work. Power refers to the rate at which that work is done. The energy in a system remains the same, but power reduces as energy becomes dissipated.

Spiritually, the practice of Raja Yoga operates in a similar way, but in an opposite direction. We re-energise ourselves by connecting to a higher power. Spiritual power has more to do with coherence and cohesion than with movement. It puts things together again and makes them whole. This wholeness has power by virtue of its truth. Like the touch of the Philosopher's Stone that turned base metal to gold, God's "touch" is His vision of the highest in us, which initiates the process of transformation.

The awakening can come through a variety of sources. Dadi Janki and many others experienced it in the early days of the Brahma Kumaris, when Brahma Baba filled them with so much power from the Supreme that they felt effortlessly transported into a state of enlightenment and bliss. People sometimes feel the same when they are with Dadi, or with others who have received so much from God that a divine sparkle shines from their eyes and face.

The "touch" can also come through an expanded state of consciousness such as described in the near-death experience, or other life crisis. Some who felt the bliss of the realm beyond – of "God's breath", as one NDE subject termed it – felt called to return to the everyday world so that they might live in a new way, and show others aspects of the deeper realities. Cancer patients and others diagnosed with terminal disease often say they only started to live once they realised they were to die.

Regaining our lost integrity

However, body-consciousness has brought a legacy of toxic ideas and beliefs that we have to face, understand and eliminate in order to become free. When we over-identified with the physical realm and forgot the soul, we developed ideas and beliefs that were protective of "I" and "mine" in physical ways but which were in conflict with our original qualities as souls. The result was that we lost our integrity, within which lies peace.

This poisonous inheritance has been causing us trouble for centuries. Sometimes it was passed on culturally, and sometimes it was carried within the soul itself. Negative (as well as positive) actions performed in one life influence our nature and character in the next.

We have to remove this poison if we are to become strong and happy, because body-conscious habits of thinking and feeling repeatedly break our connection with the divine power that can renew us. When we truly understand and connect with the Supreme, fill with wisdom, and bring the power of truth into our actions, this automatically destroys and displaces some of the dirt.

Some negative habits of thinking and feeling are long estab-lished and can be hard to shift, however. They repeatedly break our connection. So, it also takes honest self-examination to identify them and remove them.

Dadi says that the best way to do this is regularly to take time out for silent reflection.

We need to look within and see where the mind is going when it loses connection with the One, and comes into disturbance and discontentment. With regular checking, we develop more power to change.

Someone once asked me: what do you do in yoga? I replied: I clean my mirror! What will God see, when He looks at me? I want it to be a beautiful image. When we make genuine effort of this kind, it is as though God loves us even more and goes out of His way to help.

God uplifted me and showed me what a good life is.

Ego's hunger for name and fame

In Mount Abu, Rajasthan, at the original headquarters of the Brahma Kumaris, a sign hangs in the dining room that declares, "Ego is the root of all suffering". In essence, ego is the false sense of self that comes with body-consciousness, causing us to lose sight of our higher nature – the true spiritual self – and thus creating internal conflicts of loyalty that can ultimately tear us apart.

We can recognise ego by the disturbance it causes us, and usually others as well. Ego is based on conditioning, and the way our brain and limited personality work, not on the original qualities of the soul. Because it is a house built on sand, it is always insecure, and defensive.

Ego stubbornly insists it is right. It cannot bend. It causes us to become upset when other people are not behaving as we think they should. It creates jealousy, and critical attitudes. It creates a readiness to put other people down. It blocks the flow of warm, positive feelings that are original to human nature.

Sometimes ego makes us feel we must prove ourselves in the world, driving us to work ever harder to achieve social or financial status, so that we do not recognise that our lives are unbalanced. Eventually, pushing ourselves beyond the limits of our natural capacities, we will reach crisis point. Our health and relationships are both likely to fail.

Ego offers false supports to the soul. It creates ideas of racial or national superiority. It tells us that it is alright to harm or neglect others, for the sake of our own family, religion, or country.

Ego creates hunger for praise and respect, for name and fame. When this is not forthcoming, there are feelings of being insulted. When ambitions become permanently frustrated, there is anger and ultimately depression.

Cleaning the mirror

Surely, you may say, it is just part of the human condition to suffer from ego. The hungry ego, however, is not a necessary part. It is a distortion of human character, which entered our lives when body-consciousness trapped us and we forgot our divinity.

We can see that some people are heavily subject to the demands of the ego, with all the insecurity and pain that brings, while others are relatively free. That also speaks to the fact that we do not have to regard it as an inevitable part of life.

Once we learn to recognise the different forms of ego, and check regularly and honestly for where it is working negatively inside us, we can start to disempower it. The key sign is the pain it causes. The beauty of Raja Yoga is that it offers us a pure substitute for the narrow sense of self that the ego created, as well as an understanding of where ego comes from.

In the early days of the Brahma Kumaris, Dadi Janki was particularly inspired by a sister they called Mama.

She was younger than I was, but we all accepted her as our mother in a practical sense, because she was so caring and loving. Once, I asked her how she could be like that. She said it came from being able to realise her mistakes. We should understand when we have done something wrong, rather than avoid facing the fact by focusing on what others are doing.

Mama used to say that she looked after her mind very well, as if it was her child. Then it would behave well. Otherwise, it would become a vagabond, and cause trouble. She made her foundation very strong in this way.

We can think of the word realise as having "real eyes" – the eyes to see the self. When we look in a clean mirror of understanding, we can realise and change. This is an invaluable practice, which makes us valuable, because it enables us to appreciate others as well.

Clean your own mirror regularly and you will be able to see clearly how beautiful you are, as God's offspring. Fail to clean it, and you will find your mind and intellect trapped by people and situations. Look at your face in the mirror of God's heart, which reveals your weaknesses but also removes them.

Fit for life

In BK understanding, God's aim is not to obliterate our sense of self, as some religious traditions strive to do. The aim is not to strive after permanent liberation from the world, but that we should develop so much power of truth in the soul as to make ourselves fit for a return to a golden age of truth, as Brahma Baba envisioned.

Even if you cannot conceive of such a future world, you may still wish to renew your ability to live with integrity in the present day, once you have been "touched" by God to do so.

Like Humpty Dumpty, we fell off the wall and as the old English nursery rhyme says,

All the King's horses and all the King's men
Couldn't put Humpty together again.

It takes the King Himself, the Supreme Soul, to make us whole! God's vision towards us is of the highest. When we connect our minds to His, in stillness and with love, we recognise what we need to transform within ourselves. When we bring His power of peace into our actions, our lives re-integrate; they start to make sense again. Power returns to the soul.

The quality of our thoughts and feelings determines the quality of our actions, and the quality of our actions has an impact on the quality of our thoughts and feelings. Thoughts, feelings and actions filled with kindness and understanding bring benefit to others, and the good wishes others then feel towards us bring further happiness and strength.

The understanding that our identity is that of the eternal soul protects our peace, and enables us to align with God. There is that essence within, the conscious agent, who is neither the body nor its roles or relationships, but the child of the Supreme. When we restore our awareness of that pure consciousness, God and our own higher nature once again guide our life, and there is peace. It is as if the two become one, and God is able to sit in our heart.

Dadi Janki says:

I check myself, opening my heart to see if there is anyone or anything in it other than my Beloved. I want the Comforter of Hearts to reside there, so I have to be very honest in keeping the heart free for Him alone.

If you hold the determined thought that you would like the same, God will help you fulfil that aim. Internally, and repeatedly, whilst living with others, detach your consciousness from the body and bodily relationships, and remember the Father.

To move smoothly on this pilgrimage of life, we need to stay in intense love. When the soul is detached, it experiences the Father's love; and when it experiences the Father's love, it is able to be detached from the body and everything else. The soul dances. The Father's love can end all "pulls" from the world, which destroy our freedom and compromise our loving nature. Detachment means never allowing sorrow to enter the heart.

Pilgrims travel light. They learn how to drop all burdens, and they do not give burdens to other pilgrims to carry. They may travel together but they do not look behind, or wait for others who have fallen by the wayside.

If the mind keeps allowing itself to be drawn towards people and situations, it comes into upheaval and is unable to maintain the connection with God.

Facing mistakes

When a contentious situation arises in life, check how you are handling it. If it is with truth and honesty, your mind will remain peaceful and you will not become disappointed or hopeless. If you are feeling a need to speak about it a lot, with feeling, you know that cleanliness is not yet there. Honesty gives the soul so much strength that if a mistake has been made it will not be repeated.

Some people do not check in this way, and so they do not see their own mistakes but find fault with others instead. This creates ill feeling, and hardens the heart. We need to remember that however anyone is, they are a child of God.

Others take support from people or situations but are clever at suppressing awareness of their mistake, and make something look like nothing. Then they are unable to finish it. This too is dishonesty. No one can move forward based on limited support, only on what is deeply true.

If someone is dissatisfied or upset with you and you purport not to care about that person, that too is a mistake. You should not allow the situation to upset you, but maintain friendly feelings and good wishes towards the person. This pleases God! When you become pleased with the things that please God, everyone will become pleased with you.

Honesty brings a life based on truth

With God in our heart, we have everything. The power of God's love moves the soul forward, and gives strength to the body. Take His support, and you will not become confused, or your journey delayed. Understand this, and you will realise that there is no need to become caught up in other relationships. We do not need to look at anyone else's nature, or worry about what they are saying. We will care about others, but not get involved in what they are doing such that it weakens our heart's remembrance. We may have people and things in our lives, and appreciate their contribution, but not be dependent on them.

We do have to think about work and other responsibilities, but in a detached way, so that such concerns do not reduce our consciousness to ordinariness. Otherwise, when something negative happens, we will not have the strength to stay stable. By balancing mundane concerns with elevated thinking, we will stay light.

We have experienced falsehood. That was why we lost our happiness. We did not realise how bankrupt we had become. Now – what is true? This is what God is teaching us. Knowledge is light. When we keep the light of knowledge inside, negative or wasteful thoughts cannot even come close, and our nature and interactions remain sweet.

Giving and receiving blessings

Honesty means that rather than giving or receiving sorrow, our attention is on giving and receiving blessings. Blessings come from our humanity, from the soul. They are an energy, which makes us move. They are the antidote to body-consciousness, which traps us in falsehood.

The Supreme Soul creates a life for us based on truth. He is truth personified, and His energy and power flow into us when we maintain a clean and honest heart, and stay in the awareness that we are His children. Devotees remember Him as the Remover of Sorrow and Bestower of Happiness, and when we keep God with us, we become the same for others. We have everything. When we let go of His hand, our weaknesses and defects do not allow us to experience the treasure of happiness.

It is through experience that I have moved forward so much in the journey of my life. With honesty, I became free from the attraction or influence of worldly things. With Godly love, which came from awakening to who I am, as a soul, and who I belong to, my whole life changed. I received sakaash – an energy of truth, of love and light, that mends broken hearts, and makes us whole.

We have to be so honest to God that through our lives, others experience and receive the same. In this way, the merciful One puts right everything that has become topsy-turvy, and our lives become as valuable as diamonds.

"I have come as a mother"

In 1974, Dadi left India and based herself for many years in the UK. In the early days, she only had a visitor's visa and it was difficult for her to come and go.

I told the authorities, "I have not come here to make money, but for service. I have come as a mother. I want all of God's children to stay happy." Sometimes women have fear, but I was not afraid. They gave me a permanent resident's visa!

The secret of staying tension-free is to put an 'a' in front of tension – to pay attention to being an instrument, knowing that the One above is doing it all. There is no need to ask how something will happen, just to remain confident that if it is to be, then God will make it happen. To say 'I' have done something is like stealing. We are instruments for God to do this work of enabling others to understand the One.

When my spiritual sisters asked me to go abroad, I wondered what I would do there, as I did not even speak English. They told me, "Whatever you have received – happiness, peace and love – go and share that." Happiness is a treasure, and God had given me so much.

Human beings think they cannot do anything without money or position, but the basis of life is not money. I went to the UK with nothing. Honesty, love, and trust sustained me and the task. Through honesty, there is humility, and Godly power.

We need to clean up accurately at every step, dealing with issues and feelings that arise, taking what we need in terms of love or understanding, and then placing a full stop to further thought or feeling. When we keep the heart clean and true in this way, God stays in our awareness, and our attitudes and vision towards others remain pure. Through spiritual love, there are no feelings of discrimination inside based on another person's colour, caste, religion, language, and so on.

Then it becomes possible for people to receive what they need: vibrations of purity, and teachings that they can understand, learn, and experience practically. As they find success in life, they begin to have trust.

This is how the work continues. Work does not just mean a way to earn money. It is an opportunity to give happiness and good company to others. If people see that you are working with honesty and love, their hearts will accept you. I do not use the phrase, "I am responsible", but yes, I accept that having received so much, I have an obligation to share.

People often tell me that they experience the love of a mother or grandmother from me. This is not body-conscious attachment, but an inner, spiritual love that enables souls to move forward.

Chapter 9

Power of Self-Respect

Go to sleep princess, go to sleep
Go to sleep, My precious one
Sleep, princess, sleep

As truth, cleanliness, positivity and honesty re-enter our lives, self-respect also returns, in a completely natural way. Self-respect underpins almost every aspect of success in life. When we have strong self-respect, we will be generous in recognising and encouraging the expression of qualities and specialities in others. We will not dwell on their weaknesses – real or imagined – to avoid facing our own.

Self-respect removes tendencies towards jealousy and comparison. It enables us to have good wishes and pure feelings towards others. It lets us listen, without reacting, to what others have to say.

To restore true self-respect is to protect ourselves against many of the body-conscious habits of thought and feeling that cause us trouble. It enables us to overcome the negative conditioning we carried with us previously, because of living in a materialistic world in which we lost sight of the realities of spirit.

Receiving God's love

Dadi Janki teaches that the first and most vital step in the restoration of our own authentic self-respect is to recognise the deep love with which God looks at us, no matter what ugliness has entered the soul. "Can you feel that love?" she asks.

Once you have experienced it, you can have God in front of you whenever you wish, and find the courage to drop the negative self-image that obscures your inner beauty.

We need courage, because negativity, especially in the form of cynicism, is quite an old friend. It gave us a reason not to ask too much of ourselves, when our motives were mixed and we constantly risked failure as a result. When ego forms part of our motivation in action, the outcome is never satisfactory. Egotistical demands are addictive and always end in anger or tears, as we reach the limits of our coping capacity. Even when there is success, others will be very ready to accuse us of arrogance, and to try to cut us down to size.

It is not arrogance to strive to reveal our original state of perfection. God is giving us a very good explanation of how the truth and beauty with which we began our human journey became lost over time, and how we are now to regain it. The present reality is that the unchanging, ever-beautiful One, the Seed of the human family, is calling on us all to reconnect with the Source so as to renew our ability to live well, with our humanity fully restored.

To achieve that, we must let go of our past conditioning. That means refusing to listen to the voices of doubt, greed, fear, anxiety, anger and depression to which most are subject. Those voices carry power when we think of ourselves as bodily beings. Body-consciousness makes us vulnerable to the conditioned responses enfolded in the brain, and to the influence of others around us. When we consider the self to be a soul, and remember our divine Mother and Father, we fill with love and free ourselves of those influences.

We are truly wonderful

Do you feel that you are wonderful? There is absolutely no good reason why you should not, other than that you are still giving too much credence to those old voices. In one second, at every second, you can realise that God's love is absolute, and remove what is unreal inside you.

The more you clean your thinking and experience in this way, the more your awareness will shine with the beauty of reality. Focus on recognising yourself in this way, with trust, patience and determination. Let God's love be inside you. Then you will feel there is nothing to worry about – neither about the self, nor about anyone else. Everything will work out well.

Yes, the world has a myriad of problems, but to be caught up in them does not help, and is not your responsibility. We are at a special time in history when God is making eternal truth known to us and asking us to become that again, a part of the new, original consciousness – not to try to fix the old.

Compassion fatigue

Dadi says people sometimes tell her they have grown tired of being compassionate and giving love. They feel drained by their work, especially in the caring professions such as health and social services. She explains that body-consciousness drives us into worry and hurry in life, such that eventually we may become bitter and exhausted, and very aware of the mistakes of others. We need to change this habit.

When we stay in soul-consciousness, we draw divine love and power into ourselves and in that way remain loving with all, and open to correcting our own mistakes.

We need to have this care of the self. When we set such an example, others will see it and take better care of themselves. If our main concern is to serve, from the soul, as opposed to trying to prove the self to be a good or clever person, or to make money, we will not become tired. You can do business, but whatever you do, do not get busy in that!

Some people seek regard from others in everything they do, without realising it. Then they are constantly vulnerable to feeling insulted. Self-respect develops when we are free from desire.

Even if others are not respectful towards us, we should still give respect. If someone is disrespectful towards me, I do not have a bad feeling about that. I stay patient and keep serving, letting souls receive what they need, even if I do not get a response. The more I remember the qualities that lie within the self, the easier it is to be unaffected and free.

Work done with good feeling, and no selfish motive, will always bring a positive response at some point. When people realise they are receiving something real and valuable, they let go of what is false. It is a law that we must receive the fruit of our actions. However, whereas eating unripe fruit can give us pain, the fruit of patience is very sweet. If we draw respect from temporary position, honour, or money, we may be setting ourselves up for a fall.

To maintain self-respect do not expect anything of others, just accept them. When people come to me with criticisms or complaints, I always tell them: Do not judge others, judge yourself. Do not think about what others are doing. Remember that whatever you do, others will do the same. The best way to improve the behaviour of others is to set a good example.

Learn to be silent inside

We need to learn to make ourselves silent inside. Previously, many people drank water from wells at home. The water was very pure because it came from deep underground. So too, in meditation, we have to go very deep, becoming a still point. We will feel that cool, clean water is refreshing us, making both mind and body healthy. Then our compassion will not run dry.

When we are tired, we cannot give love. When we dwell on other people's mistakes, it is as if that critical consciousness weighs us down. It makes us heavy, and distances others from us. Even to say, "Oh, she is always like this" is to experience loss, because it is an act of disrespect towards the other person. Rather than dismiss them out of hand, focus on their good intentions. If you see someone sinking, reach out to them by bringing good things into their awareness, helping them not to focus on their difficulty. If we listen to them, at least our relationship will remain good.

We need faith and trust, to keep moving forward together. Continuous ups and downs can cause us to lose faith in ourselves, such that we may feel God has turned away from us, too. Even though there is so much that is good, we let one little weakness bring us down. Especially at times like that, we must maintain deep feelings of trust, in the self and God. Then after some time, it is as if God will smile and say, "The child has turned out to be a faithful one!"

There is benefit in developing a nature of acceptance. It does not mean we have to agree with others all the time, but when we give respect and regard to everyone, with truthfulness, love and faith, we receive a lot of cooperation. It does not cost us anything, does it? When it comes to wanting to give respect to others, let us have a true and big heart. This practice needs to continue over a long period.

Finding benefit

Consider everything that happens to be beneficial. Resistance is futile! What is, is. Even if it looks bad, there is always benefit within it. Work with patience, peace and love. Do not rush, or have impatient thoughts. It is when we come into our ego identities that we feel a need to prove ourselves, and become upset over obstacles. Then the spiritual outlook is difficult to maintain, and we become self-pitying and dry. Patience and humility enable us to remain peaceful.

As long as I live, I continue to learn. Even if something seems to have gone wrong, I find the lesson in it and move on with the task of bringing benefit to the world.

When honesty and love are in our words and actions, along with feelings of appreciation and friendship, others draw on this positive energy to fill whatever is lacking in them. We are able to offer them good company. Then they will give their cooperation and friendship in return. It is such a beautiful, natural process.

However, if ego mixes itself in our motives, the sound is spoiled. We need to pay a lot of attention to keeping ego away. Over-thinking opens the door to ego and spoils our value. When we think a lot, it is as if the head starts to speak without heart. Then the words are not sweet. Do not interact in a dry, tasteless manner, just for name's sake. We have to make sure that our behaviour with other people is good, as well as our connection with God.

When spirituality and Godly love are in our words and actions, we receive strength. The body stays healthy, and our connections and relationships flourish too. Others will love and respect us, because they will recognise we have something to give, rather than wanting to boost our flagging self-respect by running people down with critical comments.

Letting past be past

One who is preparing for a journey packs carefully, taking only that which is useful, and making sure he does not accumulate a burden along the way. Dadi emphasises that on our spiritual journey, we should not let our past actions hold us back. This is why the sense of having taken a new birth, with God, is so valuable.

The law of karma determines that we reap what we sow, and situations will definitely come, but with understanding, and with God as our Companion, Friend and Guide, there can be happiness at lessons learned. In this way, what might otherwise have been a crucifix becomes a small thorn.

Dadi says:

We should let the past be past – even what happened five minutes ago. To be consistently happy, we have to stop thinking about the past, and not have any desires for the future. Even if something unpleasant is happening in the present, we should not dwell on it. We are here to find solutions, not to magnify problems. Such efforts form part of keeping the heart clean and honest.

Some say they have to tolerate a lot, but this too is wrong thinking. If we gain in experience and strength from our circumstances, that is a gift to us, not a loss. If we become more tolerant, and more discerning in handling our relationships, and ourselves, it means we are overcoming weakness. Then our self-respect becomes unshakeable.

People often ask me where my energy comes from, and this is part of the answer: energy accumulates when we do not waste it. First, we take the strength to remove our weaknesses, and then we use the resulting power to resolve our problems.

A useful thought experiment is to live with the awareness of being a guest here on earth. When you are a guest in someone else's house, you do not have that sense of 'I' and 'mine' that a householder experiences. A guest is also a trustee, in the sense that he is entrusted by his host to be present in a clean and civilised way. A good guest will not make demands on his host. He will live simply, and appreciatively.

We *are* God's beloved children, and have the same qualities as the Supreme. We just have to realise and accept this truth, and the power of His love. That then makes us true inside, such that love, peace, and happiness come into our actions.

The empowered intellect

There is an art in thinking about ourselves and talking to ourselves in ways that build self-mastery, and true self-respect. Power lies in aligning our thoughts accurately to the experience of the higher self, and God.

We have seen how the intellect is a uniquely human faculty capable of discriminating between the different thoughts and feelings arising in the mind. The empowered intellect knows how to make choices as to which thoughts and feelings to embrace and nurture, and which to reject.

Education, and position, are both connected to the body. Both are assets in life if used in service of others, but weaknesses if they become the basis for our self-respect. We will suffer if we are "too clever", or if we become afraid of losing our position. Any dependency on external circumstances makes our self-respect vulnerable.

Remembering God, and contemplating the divine, bring lasting benefit to the soul. God's knowledge is of the eternal self, and the Supreme. When we hear and inculcate this knowledge, the intellect is uplifted.

Dadi Janki says:

Extraversion wastes time. Even whilst doing our work, we can keep the heart with the Beloved. We need to be introverted to maintain the divine, loving intellect that enables us to see, recognise, and know God. When there is introversion, the intellect becomes concentrated – free of external pulls. We are then able to draw into the self the power and joy of all relationships with God, as Mother, Father, Teacher, Friend, Beloved…

I made myself a companion of God, and God my Companion, by using my intellect in following the example set by Brahma Baba in achieving his own stage of perfection. He created and sustained truth in himself through a dedicated attention to subtle, non-material understanding. By keeping his intellect full of thoughts of the divine, he built self-respect in such a way that his mind and heart could stay loving and detached in all circumstances.

This state of being gives rise to a powerful vibration that is God's gift to our troubled world. It is an energy of truth. As this energy continues to spread, it will automatically restore what in India we call Ram Raj, the rule of righteousness. We do not need to think about what will happen, or how it will happen.

Faith in destiny

Pure, positive feelings bring success and powerful thoughts make the impossible, possible. Brahma Baba showed us this.

His unwavering faith in God and the benevolence of destiny enabled God to work through him. There were almost endless obstacles, but his self-respect and cleanliness of heart enabled us to pass through them all.

Say to yourself, "I am the soul, child of the Supreme. I am accepted, appreciated, and adored by God. I am a hero actor. My fall and rise are as natural as winter and spring. This body is a costume, one of many that have enabled me to play my part. It is my creation, and it reflects aspects of who I am, but it is not me. I am the eternal soul. My original nature is of love, peace and joy. Each one's part is his own, in this eternal drama of existence. There is nothing new under the sun, and nothing to worry about. The task of re-creation has already been achieved countless times."

When we talk to ourselves in this way, we fill with such self-respect that as well as transforming this life, we become a co-creator of the higher consciousness that will transform the world. The intellect becomes concentrated and powerful, and capable of being 'touched' by God as to how to act in alignment with what is needed in the world.

Contributing to divine task

When we understand and accept the love and wisdom God is showering on us, we fill with divine qualities and are able to become constantly loving with others. We need such power that when we see other people's weaknesses, it is as if we have not seen them: instead of reacting, we remain gentle and compassionate.

Practise looking at others with eyes of soul-conscious love, filled with spirituality and feelings of true friendship. Then the atmosphere instantly changes for the better. If you look in an inquisitive or questioning way, the world outside will ensnare your mind and you will no longer be able to 'see' God in front of you.

This is actually how God is creating a better world. By contributing to God's task in this way, we become master creators! Everyone now needs spiritual support. If on the other hand we are reactive, the atmosphere worsens – we are contributing to the sustenance of hell.

The power to give such authentic and profound love and respect builds inside us when, in the consciousness of being souls, separate from these bodies, we make the absorption of God's unique, divine love the central focus and purpose of our life. With God's power, our actions become powerful. It is the One above who should be praised.

Keeping the soul's original qualities in mind, we can live with strength, acting without waiting for appreciation or praise, and sharing love without allowing others to influence us or drag us down. Appreciate the unique contribution that every actor makes within the play. In each one, only a little is not so good. We need to overlook that, and constantly see their specialities. Then trust develops between us. But do not compare what others have with what you have, or you will never be satisfied.

Life is about staying light, and drawing on God's might. Then, everything becomes right! If there is a headache, it is because we have not yet developed sufficient faith in the self as God's child, and in how God is doing everything to turn the world around. World-transformation is happening through the transformation that God is bringing about in His children.

Chapter 10

Power of Silence

You are the Ocean of Love
I thirst for one drop

When people ask Dadi Janki how, in her centennial year, she can head a global spiritual university with one million regular students and 8,000 branches in 120 countries, her answer is that she is not the head, but the heart. Love and good wishes do the work.

Of course, there are decisions to be made, and obstacles to be overcome. A well-oiled administrative machine is in place, a legacy of 40 years of skilled leadership by her predecessor, Dadi Prakashmani. This deals with most day-to-day decisions. However, Dadi Prakashmani also worked primarily with the heart, and taught others to do the same. Love and respect guided her every action.

How is this possible, in a world so full of problems?

In the spaces between our actions, as well in formal contemplative practice, we can access an energy that contains both love and wisdom. When we pay attention to drawing on this energy, through moments of stillness and introspection, we create a contentment and sweetness inside that carries over into everyday connections and relationships. This sweet energy comes from a timeless dimension of reality. One feels as if one is connecting to a whole, which holds all secrets. Moreover, it is a benevolent whole, so anxiety and fear disappear and nothing but love and peace remain.

The "charge" this gives to the soul is such that it enables one to remain present to each scene that comes in front, and not caught in thinking about what has happened, or what may happen. It flows into others and helps them to work for the common good, too. In silence, there are solutions. In contrast, it is the negativity and resistance of the hungry ego that is the cause of the most intractable disagreements, as well as of individual suffering.

Different spiritual and religious traditions have given different names to this positive energy, but there is a striking commonality to the experience. Sometimes it is called the power of silence, or the power of now. Others refer to it as the peace of God. It is also known as the light, or truth, or presence. Perhaps an aspect of it is in what the Irish refer to as "the crack". The English poet William Wordsworth captured it in these lines:

...And I have felt
A presence that disturbs me with the joy
Of elevated thoughts; a sense sublime
Of something far more deeply interfused,
Whose dwelling is the light of setting suns,
And the round ocean and the living air,
And the blue sky, and in the mind of man;
A motion and a spirit, that impels
All thinking things, all objects of all thought,
And rolls through all things.

When a battery is charged, machinery that depends on it runs smoothly. If it runs low, there will be problems. It is the same with this divine energy. When we keep it with us, it produces a quality of serenity and "flow" that enables us to understand and work well with others. It frees us from our self-absorption and narrow worldly concerns. It also illuminates our lives. When it is missing, we are liable to stumble and fall.

This energy is not God, the Seed, but we can think of it as a current that flows from God. God really does "breathe" love and truth into this world. When we remember God accurately, with heart and soul, the power of that love and truth stays with us and does whatever needs doing.

This is a wonderful, worry-free way to live. It is as though we are dancing with God. He is the Lord of the Dance. We do not have to do anything – just be free to follow His lead.

As instruments in His hands, He makes us move and play. We just have to be honest in our efforts to remain present in front of Him, filled with love, and detached from worldly attractions. When we stay connected, we are able to catch His signals as to how He wants us to move, and receive the power that enables His task to be done through us. This attracts others to want to do the same. If our old nature prevents us from being a true instrument, the music will not be so sweet.

Alloy mixed in the gold

The question then arises: if this is truth, why is it so elusive? Why is there so much unpleasantness in the world? Why do we not learn how to draw on this love and wisdom in our churches, mosques, temples, homes and schools?

In fact, teachings enabling us to access the divine have always been present, although we have commonly overlooked, neglected, or misunderstood them. In the past, spiritual luminaries provided upliftment and support to millions, reminding humanity of higher truths and instructing them in ways of living that would sustain their ability to coexist with harmony and happiness.

Over time, however, as the human family grew older, its numbers larger, and its memory longer, there was an increasing loss of spiritual awareness. Our consciousness became drawn more and more to the body and the physical world around us. If we consider the original spirit of humanity to be pure gold, it is as though base metal became mixed within it. In times of peace and plenty, the kindness that is at the root of human nature could still prevail, although undercurrents of mean-spiritedness were present. When circumstances were more difficult, violence would explode.

Great religious teachers showed us the beauty and value of pure consciousness, but for many, religion deteriorated into a longing for a lost truth. Some people devoted time, energy and money to the worship of historical icons of compassion and virtue. Others found comfort in dogmas and rituals, or through blind obedience to figures of authority. Such practices sometimes gave support but ultimately became a substitute for the personal effort needed to restore truth in the self.

Institutionally, religions that once taught the unity of the human family developed divisive and narrowly self-serving doctrines instead, or became vehicles for exercising power and control.

Facing the facts

In recent times, many people gave up on religion altogether because of these failings, but in its place came ideologies, including scientific materialism, which also proved grossly inadequate. These ideologies both ignored the failings of the human spirit, and neglected its strengths.

All this has been a part of the reality of human experience. It is not something to be angry or distressed about, but a fact to be faced. Anger and sorrow take us deeper into the negative energy fields that are the very opposite of divine truth.

It takes courage to face the reality of the human condition as it is today, within the self as well as in others. When we lack courage, we hide from our weaknesses, burying them under illusory ways of thinking and behaving that provide temporary support to the psyche at the expense of deepening the darkness within us.

For a long time, that has been our story. We found a place for ourselves in the world that depended on fulfilling external conditions and social conventions. We built careers and businesses, reputations and positions, family ties and connections. It was not that any of this was intrinsically wrong, but we used these endeavours to nourish the ego, which is head-based, rather than the heart of our being, which lies within the soul.

Connecting to the eternal

Whereas the head relies on memory and learning, and is time-bound, the heart connects us to the eternal. Remove the heart from our story, and the ego becomes increasingly malignant. It makes us constant takers, unable to give; constantly hungry, and never satisfied. The defensive and selfish actions to which such an ego gives rise form a thick crust of insensitivity within. Eventually this crust surrounds the poor heart so thoroughly that we no longer realise the harm we are doing to others and ourselves.

We worship logic, and reason, but these are brain-based skills, and the brain lacks an innate sense of ethics. The conscience, which is in our heart and soul, no longer works. We lose sight of the "trespasses" we are performing. Then we cannot understand why life seems such a constant struggle. It becomes like a living death. We may gain the occasional glimpse of the love, peace and happiness that are our true nature, but to experience and express these qualities continuously seems an impossible dream.

It can feel as if we have fallen in quicksand and that the harder we struggle, the deeper we are drawn in.

Not everyone is in this plight. Some have the good character that allows them to negotiate life successfully, and the reflective skills that help to maintain their clarity and strength.

Dadi Janki says however that it has become clear from her travels all over the world that there is enough darkness and confusion to cause many to be suffering intensely. She feels passionately that just as she and many others felt reborn through the understandings and love they received from God through Brahma Baba, and learned ways to develop and sustain a renewed consciousness in their lives, others should receive the same.

She says:

Experience tells me that at this time in history, in this deep darkness, we can only receive the power to change from God. Not even God's 'breath' is enough, without an understanding of its origin, and the courage to connect to the Source itself. When we keep courage, we receive a thousand-fold return from God, becoming complete in purity, happiness and peace. This has been the basis of my life.

Seed of the human world tree

A powerful way to think about this process of renewal is to understand God as the Seed of the human world tree, and that the Seed activates at this time. In human terms, it is as if our spiritual Father, the Supreme Soul, reaches out to us. He opens His arms to us and says, "My beloved, long-lost and now-found children, come to me and I will make you whole again."

We are able to feel this loving, welcoming, empowering energy when we develop the habit of staying introverted. To the extent that we experience it, we melt inside and it feels as if the Beloved is transforming iron into gold, as the alchemists sought to do. Then, as long as we remain clean inside, we will remain safe from the illusory ways of thinking that cause our happiness to drain away. Honesty, love, and peace do the work of transformation.

This fire of yoga can finish the "well of tears" the soul has had inside for many births, enabling us to go beyond the influence of the body and to experience super-sensuous joy. In our company, others will feel able to experience the same. When we become true gold, our vibrations and example inspire others to undertake the path of transformation as well.

Whenever possible, take the opportunity to go into the depths of silence – into the depths of yourself. You will greatly enjoy the feelings of peace that come to you. In that deep peace, you accumulate power, and through that power, you create an elevated atmosphere. As those around you experience the vibrations of this atmosphere, they will bless you from their hearts.

Give yourself the experience of being fully silent, even for one minute. Ask yourself, "Who am I? Who is mine?" Adopt the awareness that you are a pure soul, free of the pull of matter, and that your Father, the Supreme Soul, is your Companion. This brings strength, enabling you to conquer selfish actions, and finishing the negativity that you are liable to experience when you keep looking at others. You will become a carefree king, feeling that God is getting everything done.

Silence enables us to become introverted, and introversion enables us to understand the value of silence. It allows us to keep God, the One who is always beyond the physical world, in front of us, and remember the fortune that we receive from Him.

Divine connection

When this awareness becomes natural, we do not have to make effort to be in soul-consciousness and then to remember God, but rather, the power of divine connection works through us in an automatic way. As this subtle link becomes well established, it enables us to live with the consciousness that God's power is working through us, and helping everything to happen. God fulfils all our pure desires when our aim is clear, and the heart is clean and honest.

This power from God makes us loving, and detached. Even while being in the body, we can enjoy a stage of being bodiless. It is as if the body is here, but the mind is there, with the Seed. We become free of everything, and within that freedom we experience a feeling of being full, completely contented, at peace, with no thoughts arising. By staying in such sweet silence, we become the embodiment of God's remembrance, and then the power of those pure, high quality feelings makes everything work well in our lives.

Raja Yoga is about a connection of the heart. When you love someone, there is no effort. Simply carry these thoughts and feelings in your heart, mind, intellect and attitude, and your life will be beautiful. When the heart is clean and truthful, the mind stays peaceful, and the intellect works well. They are all connected. When the intellect remains introverted, and focused, it becomes easy to meditate and the mind stays free of weak thoughts. It requires intelligence to know what to remember, and what to forget. If you allow waste to remain inside, that is not the life of a Raj Yogi. If you move into extraversion, you cannot experience silence.

Our thoughts are the basis of our attitude, and according to our attitude, so is our vision. We stay in God's vision by renouncing extraverted, body-conscious thoughts and behaviours, and then God becomes visible through our eyes – He gives us the capacity to take others beyond with a glance.

By bowing down, dying to our old nature, learning from God, and putting aside everything else, we become the lights of the eyes. Then we remain happy, and others are happy with us.

When we were first learning to think and feel in this way, others called it our imagination. They were not being complimentary. However, imagination in that negative sense is something unreal, and whatever is unreal will ultimately let you down. In contrast to that, we have worked with these ideas and practices now for more than 75 years, and they are enabling us to flourish both as individuals and as an organisation. I invite you to consider that we may be working with truth!

Part 3: Death

"Give up yourself and you'll find your real self. Lose your life and you'll save it. Submit to death, submit with every fibre of your being and you'll find eternal life."

– C.S. Lewis

Chapter 11

Reaping a Destiny

O Lord please show the path to the blind
I keep stumbling at every step

There is a saying, "Sow a thought, reap an action; sow an action, reap a habit; sow a habit, reap a character; sow a character, reap a destiny."

Dadi Janki has built her life on the basis that God is offering us the opportunity to reap a great destiny at this unique time in history, sharing His full love and wisdom with us in order to create a new consciousness for a new world. However, we have to respond to His call. We have to renew our thoughts, actions, habits, and character.

Can you sense, through Dadi's words, the unconditional acceptance, appreciation and even adoration that the Supreme Soul extends towards us, and how that energises renewal? Only the Supreme can offer us this energy, because from His vantage point of being eternally "off-stage" – that is, outside the world drama in which all of us are actors – God retains the entire picture. He calls Himself the Ocean of Knowledge, as well as the Ocean of Love. The knowledge held by the Supreme does not depend on any kind of cleverness, but rather, on purity consciousness.

We can regain that same purity and breadth of vision, but to become fully alive in a fresh way, we have to die to the old. It happens in three stages: dying to our old nature; to the old body; and to the old world. Finally, we become angels, beacons of light, helping others to make the same transition, from night into day.

Chapter 12

Dying to Our Old Nature

To die in your lane, to die in your lane
To live in your lane, to die in your lane
My life will be spent in your lane

The ego is a sense of self constructed within the brain, from memory. It comprises the many different components of identity that we acquire during a lifetime. Psychologists say we need a healthy ego. It gives us some parameters within which to live, which others also can recognise, enabling us to fit into the world around us.

Our problems arise because in the absence of deeper self-awareness, the ego structures take over as our sense of self. We invest so much energy into them that they become our masters, rather than servants. That is, from helping us to negotiate life, they start to make demands on us. Instead of playing our roles lightly, we begin to have to prove ourselves in a variety of ways: as men and women, as parents, as breadwinners, as citizens, as members of religions, as "good people" or tough guys, as leaders or followers – the list is endless.

There is nothing wrong with these or a multitude of other roles. The mistake was and is to confuse the role with the soul; to think that we are these roles. The result of that mistake is that over time, the role becomes ever more demanding, because we become increasingly anxious about what will happen to us if we fail to fulfil it. The greater the anxiety, the more burdensome the role becomes. Instead of bringing to the role the qualities of the true self – the lightness, love and positivity intrinsic to the soul – the role takes us over and those intrinsic qualities become increasingly hard to access.

We now have to escape from this double bind – this darkness. The reward of doing so is immeasurably great. We are able to know God, and free the spirit. Or we could say, free the spirit and know God. Either way, the key qualities needed are faith and courage. We need to understand deeply what is on offer from God, and at the same time find the courage to "die" repeatedly to the old ways of thinking and being that keep us trapped in our limited identities.

Brahma Baba's example

When the Brahma Kumaris began this work more than 75 years ago, the founding members had the advantage of Brahma Baba's immediate presence and example. His renunciation of his former life was total. He made provision for his family, and welcomed into the divine community those relatives who wished to join him in the journey of renewal, but in his mind he died to the role of limited father. He saw himself instead as father of humanity, because of the role of spiritual pioneer that God had given him.

He withstood great pressure from relatives, business associates, and religious and community leaders to abandon the teachings because of the disruption they caused to established patterns of living. He not only lost his social standing, but also became widely regarded as a pariah. News of the commotion spread across India and even as far as London and America.

Although Dadi Janki was much younger than Brahma Baba at the time and had less to lose, her part also incurred strong criticism from relatives, and required deep faith, courage, and determination. Many of the sisters, in those early years, faced intense pressures from their families to abandon their spiritual vision and aspirations, and return to living "normal" lives.

Some gave in to those pressures. "Dying" to old connections and relationships whilst still alive is not like going to your auntie's home, as the saying goes.

Today, the Brahma Kumaris are generally well respected

within India, but in other countries misunderstandings sometimes remain and there have been occasions when I too have felt the journey to be a hard one.

But it is so worthwhile! The more we understand ourselves as souls and remember the Supreme, the stronger we grow in our ability to interact positively with others. The freer we become of the demands of the hungry ego, the more we are able to see clearly the needs and qualities of others, and experience our own original, loving and peaceful nature.

Paradoxically, the more we die to our body-consciousness and interact with love and truth, the more alive we become. The joy we find in rediscovering our original power is unlimited.

How the soul changes

In the East, there is a widely held belief in reincarnation and the continuity of the soul. It tends however to be more of a comforting idea than a deeply held conviction. People think that somehow their personality and character will go on after they die, and into their next birth.

They acknowledge and understand, rightly, that our actions in this birth influence what happens to us in that next incarnation, and that according to each person's account of good or bad actions, so we will reap the fruit. However, there is also a common belief that the soul itself is immune to action. Thus, in this way of thinking, the "I" that takes rebirth, carrying with it the consequences of previous actions, would be different from the soul, which is immune to action.

In the teachings of Raja Yoga, the understanding is subtly but vitally different. We *are* souls, and although our original nature is pure and peaceful, our actions influence the soul itself so that its predispositions change. There is a similarity to the mathematical concept in physics called the wave function, which describes the range of possibilities of how a particle or physical system may manifest, and which evolves over time.

The soul begins its journey in the physical world in a state of pure being, but circumstances gradually affect it, such that other tendencies alter its original state of simplicity and purity. Some of these tendencies are negative, and some positive, depending on the life an individual leads, but they compromise the original divinity that all souls derive from our Father, the Seed.

As we take rebirth, we carry these tendencies with us. However, it is not that the entire personality or character we have experienced in one birth goes with us into the next. Much of that previous character consists of memory expressing through the brain and body. When we die physically, those memories no longer have the same hold on us, and usually fade quite soon.

When we take a new body and start developing the wherewithal for a new life using a fresh brain, with fresh relationships and in fresh circumstances, our character will differ from that of the previous birth. Nevertheless, some of the predispositions carried with us from our previous life experience will also emerge, as our new role unfolds. Each soul has a unique identity, which stamps the mind with a distinctive, though evolving, character.

Law of karma misinterpreted

This clarification is important for humanity. Losing sight of the true nature of the soul was one of the factors that led us into decline. When people fail to recognise that their actions bring long-term consequences to the soul itself, it is a misapprehension that discourages elevated behaviour, and blocks awareness of where the soul is going wrong in life.

The law of karma, that "as you sow, so you shall reap", is widely understood in India, for example, but is sometimes interpreted in such a way as to lead to a passive acceptance of the status quo, rather than as a spur to self-upliftment or improvement.

Failure to understand that the soul itself carries the consequences of positive and negative actions, rather than being immune to action, has contributed to this shortcoming. The conscience slowly dies. People think life in an imperfect world is bound to require us to act selfishly at times. They comfort themselves by thinking that a donation of some kind will help to put things right. The impact of corrupt behaviour on the soul itself is not recognised.

Three vital truths

In Western religious tradition, the idea that after death we go to either heaven or hell has similar shortcomings. Perhaps it once served as a spur to good behaviour, but it fails to convey three vital truths.

One is that as souls, all of us are God's children, "made in His image". The Supreme Father loves His entire creation, even though we differ in the extent to which we can recognise and absorb that love.

The second is that as human beings, we are actors on the world stage, playing our roles; the role is not the soul, and therefore never deserving of condemnation in God's eyes.

A third is that the play, with its movement from light into dark, from new to old, and old to new, runs eternally. At the end of the play all souls return to their home "off-stage", but that is outside space and time. We do not merge into nothingness. We retain, in a state of potential, the uniqueness of our individual human roles. Within space-time, the play is continuous.

These understandings are vital because they indicate that it is neither possible for anyone to be condemned to eternal damnation, nor to find eternal bliss or rest. Both beliefs are limiting. The first induces fear and guilt, creating chronic disturbance inside that diminishes our ability to connect to the divine. The second encourages an other-worldliness which may be comforting, but which is liable to cause us to neglect the self-transformation and world-transformation needed for the planet to be restored to its state of perfection, as it was in the beginning.

Power to make our lives worthwhile comes from understanding the full picture, and letting that awareness inform our actions.

God is doing everything

Dadi Janki says:

Looking back 80 years, my feeling is that I too was confused and wandering, separated from the Supreme Soul. God then found the soul, and made me belong to Him. Connection with God allowed me to start to understand my real nature, and to begin to die to the old. I learned to take everything from God during meditation, filling myself with patience, peace and love, to become free from desires. Then I started to understand others, and to be better able to act towards them with generosity of spirit, as God does, rather than allow negative aspects of my old nature to drive me. I found that when you really recognise the Father, you also recognise yourself.

As this strength has grown, I have felt increasingly that I am an instrument for God, acting on His directions, in a practical way. It is as if I, the child of God, receive so much from the Father as to become equal, such that His purpose can work through me. There is the feeling that nothing is mine, and that God is doing everything.

Having done any type of service, I have to leave it with my mind – throw it into the ocean, rather than take satisfaction from it. Fruit will come when it is ripe. This is an aspect of cleanliness. To think 'I' have done something is harmful to the self. Brahma Baba never said he had done anything. His attitude was that the Father was doing everything, through us.

All can share this aim. You just need to take yourself repeatedly into the awareness of being a bodiless soul, child of the Supreme, detached from everyone and everything. This is where full power lies. You become able to stabilise yourself in being humble, sincere, obedient, patient, faithful, and loving, to finish the falsehood brought about by body-consciousness, and to bring God's remembrance into your thoughts, actions, and relationships. This earns you a place in God's heart, and everything becomes easy. You become able to love and respect everyone, and to give happiness to all.

People sometimes tell me that they have understood the need for love, and truth, but find it difficult to stay positive when they share their lives with others who are persistently needy and demanding. I tell them: God, the Father, is in my heart. I allow nothing else in.

Do not waste time. Make up your mind that this is what you want, and you can do the same.

Chapter 13

Leaving the Body

O Traveller from afar, take me along with You
Take me along with You

J. Krishnamurti, the renowned Indian philosopher and teacher, wrote that "To understand death, you have to understand life. But life is not the continuity of thought; it is this very continuity that has bred all our misery."

There is deep wisdom in this comment. Much of Krishnamurti's life's work was concerned with helping others to understand the quality of mind that enables us to be truly alive, not living in the past. He had great insight into the beauty of bringing death into every moment of living, by living with soul intelligence and ending our attachment to the transitory and impermanent.

Soul is deeper than thought. Thought is brain-based, and conditional. Soul originates from God, and is eternal. When we identify with our thinking and opinions, we are identifying with something that is already dead – a memory, a dream. As we make the shift to soul-identity, we become fluid, and free.

Death of a lawyer

The Russian writer Count Leo Tolstoy had this understanding, and wrote a magnificent short story, *The Death of Ivan Ilyich*, which illustrated it. It was about the life and last days of a successful lawyer. Ivan Ilyich was intelligent, good humoured and sociable, but strict in doing what he considered to be his duty – which meant what was expected of him by those in authority over him. He became an examining magistrate, married a girl appropriate to his social position, and set up home with an eye to what would impress his friends. Everything seemed to be going along well.

Soon after the marriage, however, his wife started to become irritable and demanding. Instead of being able to find out why, he retreated more and more into his official duties. For as long as he kept climbing the career ladder, the years went by acceptably – for him; but after being passed over twice for promotion, his world started to fall apart and his health went into a steep decline. He died aged 45, having screamed "incessantly", according to his widow, for three days and nights.

The beauty of the story lies in the insights we gain during Ilyich's last hours. It gradually dawns on him that he had not spent his life as he ought; that all he had lived was a "horrible, vast deception". He resists the realisation at first, feeling hatred towards his wife, and more physical and mental agony than ever. Two hours before his death, as he is struggling against being pulled into a "black sack", as he experiences it, his son takes his hand, kisses it, and bursts into tears.

At that very moment, Ilyich glimpses a light, "and it was revealed to him that his life had not been what it ought to have been, but that that could still be set right".

'Yes, it has all been not the right thing', he acknowledges, and asks himself, 'What is the right thing?' At last he feels sorry for his wife and son, and realises he must act so that they might not suffer – to set them free. He tries to say sorry, but when the words will not come out right, he shakes his hand, "knowing that He would understand whose understanding mattered".

The pain suddenly becomes something distant, and his old accustomed terror of death disappears. "There was no terror, because death was not either," Tolstoy writes. "In the place of death there was light."

Ilyich's death is redeeming, but how much better to learn to *live* with that compassion and peace, and the forgiveness that makes compassion possible, so that we can approach the end of our lives with ease, and without fear. When we practise and maintain the awareness of "Who am I?", as a soul, and "Who is mine?", as the beloved child of the Father, we carry with us in our lives the awareness of the virtues and powers we receive from God, including peace, love, and knowledge of the whole picture.

God's intelligence

If we think too much, we cut ourselves off from God's intelligence. Then our intellect shakes, and our happiness diminishes. If we let the past be past, and make big situations small, and see the good in all, our living and dying are continuous, and beautiful.

Two big enemies of such living and dying are ego and attachment. These subtle vices easily creep up on us unrecognised, as they did with Ivan Ilyich. Deliberate inculcation of humility helps us to remain free, and stay in the feelings of our humanity.

Humility comes when we leave the "I" of body-consciousness, and through self-realisation come to know God, and make God our companion. Then there is never the feeling that we are alone, or in need. "God is mine, and I am God's". So there is no room for arrogance.

Quiet, incognito, internal effort is needed for this, Dadi Janki says. "Rehearse it throughout life. Then when the moment comes when we most need humility – which could be in illness, or in death, or in some other real or threatened loss – we will stay free."

Tolstoy's story also shows how people adopt different forms and play different roles in order to impress others, but that the deeper reality may be utterly different. To be real, whilst living in a world of illusion, we need to stay in the consciousness that we are souls, lost in the love of the Supreme. In the awareness of our eternal form as bodiless souls, we become free of the need to try to be something else.

Pull of love

When we go deep into soul-consciousness, we feel naturally detached from the body and physical relationships. We feel the pull of love from divine light, and from the One above. That experience enables us to stay in this world, with an attitude of detachment. The soul receives power from God, so that we can leave our old nature, which used to make us victims of the vices that were the root of our suffering. The heart starts to "feel" the One who is transforming the soul.

Soul-consciousness also weans us away from the habits of questioning, criticising and complaining about others. We recognise that each one is a soul, playing their unique role. A play requires a big variety of actors. It does not matter what weakness someone else has. That is his or her part. Perhaps we can show them so much love and happiness that they transform. As our own selfishness diminishes, we can give true love, which changes the atmosphere. It is actually God's love, with which we have become aligned.

Ivan Ilyich learned generosity of heart at the last minute, after three days of intense suffering. If we learn to experience it as of now, through the loving link with God, our actions and relationships will become positive and peaceful and we will feel deep gratitude towards the One who has taught us how to live.

Dadi Janki says:

Understand and experience this inner link. Keep the determined thought to maintain it, leaving or transforming whatever gets in its way, and you will receive everything. Every aspect of your life will become as valuable as a diamond. Then when the time comes, you will slip away from your body as easily as a snake sheds its skin.

I have no fear of death. God taught me how to die alive, such that I am ready at each moment for the journey home. He has given me this lift, so that I can travel easily in His company. He taught me good actions, so that I could become relieved of past burdens. I also know that in the golden age to come, there will be no such thing as premature or untimely death. We will all leave our bodies with ease, sensing the right time to move on.

I have been with many souls when they left the body. It is good to think in advance about how you will leave. If, now, you are always busy, what state will you be in when you reach your final moments?

We should remain easy, rather than rushed, confused and stressed, because any moment may be our last. We should not accept sorrow, even if someone tries to give it, and we should not do any actions that cause sorrow. All such habits affect our yoga, damaging our ability to maintain the consciousness of the soul and the Supreme, and bringing us into limitation.

If we hold a negative impression of another, we will definitely not be able to inspire them to move forward. In fact, we should not allow other human beings to influence our thoughts either positively or negatively, because of either liking them or not liking them. Rather, let us hold a vision of appreciation for what each one does. That brings happiness.

If we live in happiness, we will die in happiness. If our hands are always giving, always bestowing, joy will be ours in death as well as life.

It is not necessary to think in ordinary ways, to worry or to ask questions. Those are all habits connected with the physical identity, formed during our experience within this tired old world. See those habits now as out of date, and of no more value to you. Go into the depths of One, with an honest heart, and enjoy a stage of such lightness and mastery that nothing of the external world, even the body, can influence you against your will.

Chapter 14

Dying to This Old World

The Lord is standing at your door
O bhagat fill your apron

"Dying is nothing to fear. It can be the most wonderful experience of your life. It all depends on how you have lived." So wrote the late Elisabeth Kübler-Ross, the Swiss-American psychiatrist who both cared for and interviewed thousands of patients who were either dying, or had a close brush with death.

She received a conventional western medical education but later became convinced that the ultimate source of the universe's energy is pure love, that in our form of spiritual energy we are love, and that to learn to love unconditionally is the highest goal in life. A pioneer in the study of the near-death experience, she found that people who have died clinically and then come back to tell the tale report experiencing a life-changing "epiphany of thought". Sometimes this involved prophetic warnings and insights, and a feeling of being "surrounded by every bit of knowledge there was, past, present and future". For everyone, there was a bright light, radiating warmth, which "taught them that there is only one explanation for the meaning of life, and that is love."

Dr Kübler-Ross was especially well known for her theory that our coming to terms with major losses, and especially impending death, can be considered as taking place in five phases. In her model, the first likely response is denial of the reality of the situation. When that is no longer sustainable, anger often follows, and then a phase she called "bargaining" in which the individual hopes some deal can be done with life, or God, that will mitigate the loss. Fourthly, as the reality of the loss sinks in,

115

there can be depression, until finally there is acceptance and a readiness to move on.

An end and a beginning

Please now bear with me, dear reader, as I ask you to consider the possibility that humanity as a whole is currently experiencing the different stages of grief described by Elisabeth Kübler-Ross. Her model may help us better understand, as a global family, events now taking place in the world which may signify the deepest aspect of loss in our history, which can also be our greatest opportunity.

From the start of the Brahma Kumaris movement in the mid-1930s, it was the founder's conviction that the world as we have known it for millennia is soon to end. He received visions of almost intolerable intensity of a global destruction in which earthquakes, floods, missiles and civil war would cause everyone to die to this physical existence.

Subsequently, he saw the re-emergence of a world of unity and love, peopled by human beings so fresh and pure in their spiritual energy and awareness as to be termed deities.

Drawing circle after circle on a wall at a friend's house in Benares, Brahma Baba envisioned us all as actors in an eternal drama that plays out on a wheel of time, such that the end gives rise to the beginning. He felt God was showing him that the play is now entering just such a period of transition, in which the old would give rise to the new. For the new deity world to become manifest, a new consciousness needed to be put in place in the midst of the old.

In time, he understood the task of global transformation to be the responsibility of the Supreme Soul, the Seed of the human family, and that its success is guaranteed. Since God is bodiless, however, and beyond the material world, human beings have to make the effort to change. They are able to renew the power of pure consciousness in themselves when they understand themselves to be souls, not bodies, and learn to have unadulterated remembrance of the Supreme. Through that remembrance, the power of truth within the Seed will once again manifest within the world.

At the end of the play, souls will return to their home, a region of absolute peace that exists outside time and space. Then as the cycle of time unfolds once more, we will come to play our parts according to our eternal place in the drama of existence.

Unchanging totality of existence

So truly, we are immortal, not just in the sense that the soul somehow lives on when the body finishes. There is just the one cycle, an unchanging totality of existence, which plays eternally and so within which our roles on the stage are eternal as well.

The insights that came through Brahma Baba in those early days have a bearing on age-old controversies, including the seeming contradiction between predestination, sometimes argued for by physicists as well as theologians, and our sense of free will. The understanding of a cycle of time that repeats identically as well as eternally enables us to see that as conscious, living agents, we do choose how we perform, but also that our choices become "set" for all time as we make them.

The human family forms a tree that grows throughout the duration of the play. The trunk represents a unified world, in which pure spiritual awareness enables us to live in unbroken harmony and happiness with each other, and with the elements. The population is relatively small in that era.

As the cycle of time progresses and the tree grows bigger, that original unity is lost. Nevertheless, great branches of religious belief and practice form, inspiring millions to strive to live in ways that bring them closer to God, and to one another.

Importance of the present time

Brahma Baba's visions, as well as the suffering and ignorance he saw in the world around him, gave him a sense of urgency and immediacy concerning the task of world renewal.

He felt that the human family was entering a period of confluence between old and new, and that he was being called upon by the Supreme to lead the renewal of consciousness that would bring the new world into being.

Although eventually he was to state that this confluence would last about 100 years, those who joined him in the task of renewal lived from the start with the idea that there was no time to waste in making the changes needed inside themselves to bring the pure new world into being.

It was a sense of the imminence of global transformation that led Brahma Baba to make such a dramatic change of direction in his life, disposing of his business and entrusting a core group of young women with the proceeds in order to enable the founding members of the spiritual university to live and work together.

Whilst fulfilling responsibilities in relation to his immediate family, he rapidly let go of the body-conscious attitudes and behaviours that pull the mind and intellect and block our connection with God. He did this so powerfully that he became an instrument for God's task. A divine power entered him, guiding his actions and inspiring others. He always attributed this power of love and wisdom to the Supreme.

Those who recognised this divinity felt a similar sense of urgency, which became a spur to their effort.

Dadi Janki says:

We discovered that the more we let go of old ways of thinking and connecting, the more the love, peace and happiness intrinsic to the soul were able to inform and uplift our lives. In the 14-year period when we lived as a 300-strong community in Karachi, it was as if we were already dead to our old, limited selves.

When we moved to India in 1950 and began to share the teachings across the country, the people we met often felt as though angels had come among them.

Restoring pure spiritual love

Over the decades since, we have put a great emphasis on freeing others and ourselves from body-consciousness, and restoring spiritual love in our relationships. We have created a global network of meeting places and retreat centres that offer opportunities for the practical experience of soul-consciousness, and of the positive, transformational power we can bring into our present lives through accurately understanding the Supreme and making Him our companion in action.

As the years have passed, the unsustainability of present-day reality has pressed itself more and more forcefully into human awareness.

In the mid-1930s, when the Brahma Kumaris began, scarcely more than two billion people were here on earth. Today, the figure is approaching eight billion. Advances in science and technology have made this expansion possible, but at enormous cost.

The planet is suffering severe environmental degeneration. Climate patterns are changing. The oceans are losing oxygen, acidifying, and warming as they absorb heat trapped on earth by greenhouse gas emissions. Fish stocks are dwindling. Many animal species are disappearing. Forests, the lungs of the earth, are shrinking. Water supplies and energy resources are under pressure. Pollutants have reached everywhere.

Even if none of these environmental pressures existed, a huge arsenal of nuclear weapons is still in place, capable of devastating the entire earth in seconds.

Anger and denial

Some of those who have awoken to these crises become angry that governments and other people so often seem to be in denial about the reality of the situation. They become aware after a while, however, that this anger and frustration can compromise both their health and their effectiveness.

Perhaps it would be useful for us to see anger, as well as denial, in this context of global destruction as among the natural signs of the process of grieving described in the "five-phase" model.

Even the "bargaining" that is going on – the hopes that something can be salvaged from the mess, despite expert reports telling us it is already too late – may be seen in the same light.

It is as if we sense our world is in a terminal condition, but because of our lack of information about the bigger picture (including the fact that ultimately death does not exist) we find the thought of leaving it impossible to bear. It is difficult to contemplate loss without the understanding or hope that something much better may come in its place. If loss is imminent, however, and we do not face up to it and prepare for it, we will be setting ourselves up for a big and painful shock.

A never-ending story

Dadi Janki says:

This may be why I have lived as long as I have – to share with as many as I can my conviction and vision that just as the death of an individual should be understood as a transition, the same is true about the terminal afflictions facing life on earth. The world does not need our worry or sorrow.

We are part of a never-ending story, an unbroken whole. There is nothing to fear but fear itself, and fear disappears when we realise we are actors in an eternal play. Now it is as though we are enacting the finale, with nearly all the actors present, and preparing for our final bow.

The time is approaching when we will leave the stage and our physical costumes, and return to our place of origin, our sweet spiritual home beyond space and time. To prepare for that homecoming, we have to immerse ourselves in God's love and become detached from the world.

This understanding, and the awareness of the home, has underpinned my life. There has been so much benefit experienced through it. Until we receive the knowledge of the drama, we cannot remain fully soul-conscious. Knowing that this world has to change, and that it is time for each soul to prepare to return home, gives strength to our efforts to stay in remembrance and become free of subservience to the vices. Then we become ones who distribute happiness!

By remaining introverted, with God, I developed a power of concentration that enabled me to live in this old world with great peace and happiness. It has been as if God is my world, and I have had nothing else to do but stay in the feeling of belonging to one Father, and none other; and of all souls being brothers. Such an attitude has enabled me to stay beyond any type of worldly influence or attraction.

I think to myself that things are neither good nor bad, and that what is important is to hold on to the nature of not being drawn into issues and events. Whilst living in the world, I hold the awareness that it has lost strength and truth, and is finishing. My task is to make myself ready for the new world.

The method is simply to remember the Father, knowing that whoever and whatever I am or have been, I belong to Him.

Then I can stabilise in the consciousness of being beyond the body, and the peace and power of the Creator come on to my face and into my actions and relationships, inspiring each of the people I meet to move forward. I have spiritual love for everyone.

You too can go into the depths of this subtle, Godly love, and others will experience spiritual love through you. This is my one desire, that everyone should receive what I have received, and free themselves from the mire of weakness and all negative omens.

The sign that you have filled with truth and love is that nothing wasteful can enter you, or even scratch you. There is no place for it. By connecting the intellect with God over a long period, not letting it dangle in anyone else's remembrance, and so experiencing only pure, positive, determined and powerful thoughts, it is as though your mind becomes like a diamond.

Death as a taboo subject

In poor countries, death is an ever-present reality that is hard to ignore. In many parts of the economically developed world, however, it has been a taboo subject and we have not been handling it well. Too often, we ask doctors and hospitals to fight to keep dying patients going after their quality of life has steeply deteriorated, sometimes spending huge sums on keeping souls in bodies for just a few last days or weeks. In England, more than half of all deaths take place in hospital even though this is the location least preferred by patients.

When our internal "map" of reality tells us we are physical beings and that everything ends with the body, death may seem like the ultimate tragedy and its postponement a top priority. Our lives seem such a waste, except for the memories we have left in the minds of the living.

When we realise death is illusory, in the sense that the essence of our being never dies, it loses its sting. When we understand that on leaving these bodies we may find ourselves in a condition of primal bliss, death may even seem attractive. When we learn that we play our parts eternally on the stage of the world, and that the way we leave our bodies now creates a trajectory for the soul's future, we see the importance and value of leaving in soul-consciousness, carrying all the powers and virtues God has given.

Elisabeth Kübler-Ross's work contributed to a revolution in care of the dying. It helped further the hospice and palliative care movements, and the notion of death with dignity. Her ideas about the continuity of life after death were unacceptable to many of her medical and scientific colleagues, but enabled millions to find more meaning in the experience of death and dying.

Palliative care focuses on relieving and preventing the suffering of patients, emotional as well as physical. As well as easing the dying process, it improves the quality of life both for patients and for families facing serious or chronic illness. Palliative care doctors find that it can enhance the effectiveness of conventional medical treatment, too, and increase lifespan.

Perhaps that is what has happened to Dadi Janki. Ill health dogged her for most of her life, but at the time of writing she is still going strong, after nearly 100 years. She does not have any worries about dying.

"When your life has been lived well," she says, "your death becomes easy. I learned to connect with the One, and enjoy the safety and security of keeping my mind beyond. With nothing and no one else in my heart, I am free. There will be plenty of people to look after things when I go. If we use time well, through receiving from God and sharing happiness and truth with others, there will be great happiness at the end."

Time to return home

If humanity were to adopt a "palliative" approach to caring for the planet and its people, accepting that its condition is critical and dropping our anger and denial, perhaps that may both ameliorate suffering and even prolong the "patient's" active life.

Nevertheless, we should understand that like over-tired children who have been playing for hours on a summer's evening and do not want to hear that it is bedtime, we feel resistance to the call from the Supreme to return home. We should understand the depths of ignorance into which our long journey has taken us. We have to finish our attachment to the dust and dirt of the physical world, knowing that after our rest, we will return to live another long and glorious day.

Dadi says:

Things are going to change. The world will be transformed. Our task is to remain in the consciousness of being a bodiless soul, lost in the love of God.

I made God my friend, and have His constant companionship in my life. This has cleaned me, and given me the strength to be honest in my actions. It has brought me great happiness.

All we have to do is receive. If we remain simple, we will receive everything we need. Many situations will present themselves, but when we become still, and introverted, we can learn from events and be stable. The mind becomes peaceful, and the body cool and calm.

Pure, positive thoughts bring us peace. Thoughts that spring from body-conscious desires bring peacelessness. It is this simple.

When our thoughts are powerful, so that we are uninfluenced

by people and situations, God stays present with us and we will never be defeated. Our self-respect stays intact. Then we can interact with everyone with peace and love.

I feel that the very basis of my life has been not to remember what happened yesterday, or even in the last minute. I have only to think about what I have to do now.

Do not remember your mistakes, or the mistakes of others. Be truthful, and learn to trust. Then, as God's companion, you will be able to leave all old habits, including your habitual attachment to this body and this tired old world. You will feel that you are living a beautiful life … an everlasting life. You will know the beauty of creation, and your part within eternity.

Chapter 15

Becoming an Angel

Let's fly away O bird
This land has distanced itself from us

The study and practice to which Dadi Janki has given her life enable a person to become very elevated. Not in the sense of being superior, but of being able to serve. "When we take the sustenance God is giving, we not only feel that 'I belong to God' but also that 'God belongs to me'", Dadi says. "To have the Supreme Soul at your side is no small matter." It means you have the strength to rise above being emotionally reactive to people and situations. Consequently, you have the power to be pro-active, or creative – to help find solutions. This is the special need of this time.

In the Brahma Kumaris understanding, as the cycle of time continues to turn, humanity will once again experience the pure, golden-aged world with which the cycle began. Then, there will be no problems demanding solutions.

Right now, however, there is a huge need for the presence of angels.

Angels have been well remembered in the Christian tradition as a gift from God. They are usually thought of as messengers or guides, sent by or emanating from God in order to help human beings at critical times.

There is another way of thinking about angels, which involves the understanding that with God's help, we human beings can become so free from the attraction of the body and material world as to become available to uplift others in an unlimited way. When the soul becomes deeply aware of its subtle form of light – the "blueprint" of the perfect embodied form – it can be present for others mentally, in a way that transcends normal physical laws. Angels stay above, even whilst still connected with the world. They are not aloof, but they have taken so much strength from the Supreme that they are untouched by the worry, fear and sorrow afflicting those whose consciousness is trapped in matter. Their state of freedom allows them to "be" part of the solution, lifting the minds and hearts of others out of despondency.

Through fullness of heart, and divine understanding in their intellect, angels reflect a Godly perspective on events. As we have seen, God's vision of the highest within us directly influences the material world as well. As we open up to love, letting go of habitual negativities, we restore our own loving nature to its full expression, and that has an impact both vibrationally and through our actions.

Awareness of our divinity

Dadi says:

> The way this has happened in my own life has been to know and to love God, the incorporeal One, completely, and to "die" to the body and all physical relationships. This took honesty, and courage. The result was that I received God's help, in enabling the Brahma Kumaris to reach where they have today across the world.

> To become so free, we need to die to such a degree that not a trace of our old existence remains. It is as with a cremation ceremony when even the ashes are scattered, in wind or water, so that no pull should remain between the relatives and the one who has gone.

> It is true that I learned to love God through Brahma Baba, a human being, but Brahma Baba was able to invoke the

127

presence of the Supreme so powerfully that he taught us how to know and love that One beyond. It is not a matter of belief in God, but of knowing and experiencing the self in relationship to God.

Brahma Baba made such sacrifice of his own mind, body and wealth to God as to become complete, thus enabling the Supreme to work through him. He had a unique role: God showed him his own original form of perfection, and he dedicated the rest of his life to restoring that original beauty in himself. He achieved this fully, such that even after he left his physical body in 1969, his body of light continued to serve. The spiritual university did not collapse, but went from strength to strength. The powers of purity, and yoga, enabled great expansion, within India and then globally.

When we have understood that we really are loving beings, and that the other tendencies we have acquired are distortions of the truth about ourselves; that we are part of a family of souls, under God, who is eternally full of the energy of truth that we have lost; and that now is the time for souls to regain that truth – when we feel in our hearts that this is who we are, and who we belong to, and what we now choose to restore in our lives, it is as though it has already happened. However, it has to be much more than an idea, or even an understanding. It has to be felt deeply, because the experience *is* the change.

Effortlessly, as we return repeatedly to the awareness of our divinity, it re-enters our lives. The only effort is to keep remembering, and not slip back into forgetfulness.

Thinking less, loving more

This practice of "remembrance", and the powerful experience of yoga that flows from it, changes not only the physical brain but also the field of subtle energy within which we live, a field that extends far beyond the brain. In this way, other souls receive light from afar. In fact, there is a reciprocal effect: the less we allow our consciousness to be brain-based, the more far-reaching and angelic our minds become. The less we think, the more we love.

This does not mean we become brainless. Rather, it is as if remembrance re-programmes the brain, such that it serves the higher-order aspects of our being. Remembrance forms a bridge between body, mind, soul and the Supreme.

As love renews every aspect of our being, it is as though divine purpose motivates our actions, rather than the narrow self-interest associated with body-consciousness. We have spiritual, loving feelings whilst acting and coming into relationship with others. Then it does not feel as if we are doing anything, but rather, that God's love is enabling everything to happen.

The freer we become from any feeling of obligation or bondage to others, the more there is the feeling that the Father has tied us in the bondage of His love, such that there is no longer a separation. He shows us what we must do and with Him as our Companion, our roles unfold easily and automatically.

Shedding negative tendencies

The ego is always questioning, worrying, wondering – holding on. When we die to it, and focus on accumulating power in the soul, we are able to find benefit in everything that happens. Pure thought and action reinforce internal change. The soul itself gradually sheds the negative tendencies that have been the source of so much trouble in the past.

Dadi is fond of saying that we should take three tablets every day: of patience, peace, and love.

Keeping these in your head and heart, you will stay healthy and make everything easy. Always look first at your heart, and your head, and *then* act, so that you come into relationships with those feelings.

The beauty of this way of living is that the more we die to attachments and desires relating to this material world, the freer we become to live according to our heart's deepest desires. We become free to love unconditionally. We become free of fear, worry, and unhappiness. We conquer the mind and physical senses and become a garland around God's neck, free from all other desires.

Angels are patient, humble, and sweet. They have a warm heart, and a cool mind. The heart feels warm when there is love, and the mind becomes peaceful when it stops wandering around looking for love.

If you want to make your heart warm and your mind cool, just place your hand on your heart and think about how fortunate you are to know God. The mind is not going to say anything!

In the world, lack of love has caused many barriers to arise between people. There is so much discrimination – of colour, language, religion, status, and so on – with consequent fighting and quarrelling. Because of this, the heart has suffered damage and the mind has experienced sorrow.

Working together

We want to see change, but cannot change the world on our own. We have to perform actions together. When, as yogis, we have the Supreme Soul as our Companion in life, we no longer allow the scenes that come to push and pull us hither and thither. We become detached, in a positive way, as observers of the great drama of life enacted in front of us.

We do not need to hide ourselves away in a corner, but come naturally and easily into relationship and connection with others, because we have God's love and wisdom guiding us at every step. It becomes easy for us to see other people's virtues and to be oblivious of their defects. They receive benefit from this strength, too, and when we see ourselves working together harmoniously, this brings us great joy.

Angels fly beyond once they have done their work with others. They remain free from ego and attachment. Where there is purity, there is peace, and where there is peace, there is love. Where there is love, there is happiness, and where there is happiness, there is power. Look at your heart and mind, to see to what extent these qualities are present.

Vibrations, as well as actions, transmit these benefits. In the early days of our movement, many people received visions of Brahma Baba's angelic form of light. As time goes on and many more practitioners of the yogi way of life achieve this pure state of being, people the world over will sense the presence of angels, helping them to let go of the suffering linked to body-consciousness and experience their own form of light. Such experiences will play a vital part in facilitating a forthcoming global transformation.

Would you like to contribute to that task? It is a decision you have to take. Keep in your awareness, "I have to become an angel". It needs to happen now, such that you become free of fear and animosity over a long period, and accumulate spiritual power. If you become clear that this is what you want, God will make it happen. However, rather than take a little and mix that with limited, human desires, you have to really give yourself to Him.

MANTRA
BOOKS

We publish books on Eastern religions and philosophies.
Books that aim to inform and explore the various
traditions, that began rooted in East and
have migrated West.